(s i c k)

(s i c k)

A Cultural History

of Snowboarding

Susanna Howe

St. Martin's Griffin / New York

Photographers: Chris Brunkhart, James Cassimus, Jeff Curtes, Rick Davis, Jared Eberhardt, Bud Fawcett, Stefan Fiedler, Trevor Graves, Gregg Greenwood, Justin Hostynek, Andrew Hourmont, Ari Marcopoulos, Peter Mathis, Eric Matthies, Markus Paulsen, Hubert Schriebl, Aaron Sedway, Patty Segovia, John Sposeto, Rich Van Every

(sick): A Cultural History of Snowboarding

Copyright © 1998 by Susanna Howe

Cover design by Mike Mills

Book design by Richard Oriolo

ISBN 0-312-17026-2

First St. Martin's Griffin Edition: February 1998

10 9 8 7 6 5 4 3 2 1

Books are available in quantity for promotional or premium use. Write to Director of Special Sales, St. Martin's Press,

175 Fifth Avenue, New York, N.Y. 10010, for information on discounts and terms, or call toll-free (800) 221-7945. In New

York, call (212) 674-5151 (ext. 645).

CONTENTS

ACKNOWLEDGMENTS

This book is dedicated to those who did not cop an attitude: Brad Steward, for his advice and support; Lee Crane, for his wit and confidence, and *Snowboarding Online*, for the house in Tahoe; Shanti Sosienski, Alison Berkley, Seth Neary, Noah Brandon, Sabrina Sedheghi, Gary Henderson, Martha Harkey, and Ammon Haggerty, for their comfy floors; Jeff Curtes, for always calling me back right away; Mike Olson, Pete Saari, and Paul Ferrel, for the office and a great early season; Twist, Wave Rave, Burton, Lib Tech, Switch, Yang, and Glissade for product; Mt. Bachelor, Mt. Hood, Steven's Pass, Crystal Mountain, Mt. Baker, Sta Fe Ski Basin, Vail/Beaver Creek, Alpine Meadows, Squaw Valley, Kirkwood, Donner Ski Ranch, and Stratton, for lift tickets; *SIA, Transworld Snowboarding, Snowboarder, Medium, Fresh and Tasty,* and *Blunt,* for magazines and information; Chuck Barfoot, Chris Brunkhart, Jake Burton, Jeff Curtes, Jared Eberhardt, Bud Fawcett, Trevor Graves, Gregg Greenwood, Justin Hostynek, Ari Marcopoulos, Eric Matthies, Mike Olson, Markus Paulsen, Chris and Bev Sanders, Aaron Sedway, Patty Segovia, Tom Sims, Rich Van Every, for amazing photos; Tamsin Murray-Leach, for research help; Kip Kotzen and Dana Albarella, for getting the book made; and Mike Mills for the cover and endless stashes of patience and intelligence.

The bottom of the half-pipe, US Open, 1996. PHOTO JEFF CURTES.

INTRODUCTION

SICK: (INAPPROPRIATELY, UNBELIEVABLY) COOL/DIFFICULT/SMART/INVENTIVE.

SNOWBOARDING HAS BURST INTO OUR LIVES AND BECOME A VESSEL OF MEANING FOR KIDS, MARKETERS, MEDIA, AND ADVERTISERS AROUND THE WORLD. IN 1996, 3.7 MILLION PEOPLE WENT SNOWBOARDING IN THE UNITED STATES FOR MORE THAN ONE DAY, MAKING IT THE FASTEST GROWING SPORT IN AMERICA. WHAT'S THE APPEAL? FOR THOSE WHO RIDE, IT IS SOMETHING ELEMENTAL THAT DEFIES DESCRIPTION. TRYING TO talk about it is like trying to explain why you like your favorite song. It feels good. It makes you happy. To snowboarders, snowboarding is not a book. It's not a symbol or a fashion or an attitude either. It's an awesome, personal experience that's better left unarticulated.

My own relationship to snowboarding started way back in December of '95, when I first tried what my mom refers to as "flying in the face of God." Snowboarding was taking New York by storm. Ride Snowboards was the hottest ticket on the Stock Exchange. The term "extreme" had become a catchword for advertisers, selling cars and phone service to an increasingly "edgy" audience. Fashion and music magazines picked up on snowboarding's growing popularity with "the kids," and redefined its glamour for a wider audience. Snowboarding was the ultimate concept, signifying youth, freedom, glamour, and the future; rebellion against the established and relief from the mundane. Snowboarders were alternately praised as negotiators of the future by zeitgeist-watchers and damned as degenerate derelicts by the old or uninitiated.

I myself was wary of snowboarding's trendiness. When I finally decided to do it, I felt like a fashion slave, like I had huge quotation marks around my head. But I was writing about skateboarding for a magazine in New York and it seemed important that I at least try snowboarding. Besides, I thought it would do me good to get out of town for a weekend.

It was a short and violent baptism. My first weekend snowboarding, I got a speeding ticket on the way up and totalled my parents' car on the way back. The next weekend, when I caught a ride to the mountains to try it again, I broke my shoulder. It was all very tragic, but I really didn't care. All the concerns about being trendy had faded the first time I strapped both of my feet to the board, gave my friend Phil the thumbs-up sign, stood up, and pointed straight down the baby slope. Speed, creativity, style, physical exhaustion, nature, fresh air, all of these things drew me in. It was absurd how fun it was, and you couldn't intellectualize it—you literally had to feel it work. It was a completely visceral experience, the breed of which I had figured was illegal over the age of 15. Snowboarding changed me forever. Crashing the car and breaking my shoulder only served to demarcate life before snowboarding from life now.

As things speed up at the end of the century, American popular culture is increasingly fluid and hybrid, changing fast and crisscrossed with all sorts of subcultures. Snowboarding exemplifies this process. It has evolved rapidly, shifting underneath every time the top got heavy, drawing from different sports technologies, fashions, and cultures. While the majority of new snowboarders in recent years have been attracted to the sport's cool image, time was when snowboarders were attracted to its small, inclusive community. Now, with every-one and their mother out there snowboarding, plus the distinctly un-alternative Olympic image thrown in this year, the original, warm and fuzzy associations are fading away. In other words, snowboarding has hit the mainstream. It's is no longer an identity-forming image, it's just something that people do.

How did it come to this? How did the public perception of snowboarding evolve from its origins as a supermarket toy, a gimmick much like the Hula-Hoop, to a full blown medal sport in the Olympics? The story is dynamic to say the least. Spanning the '70s, '80s, and '90s, snowboarding has developed its own culture, complete with an evolving set of values. These are reflected in music, fashion, art, graphics, and attitude. The time is right to look back at the first thirty years and examine snowboarding as an example of a subculture's evolutionary process: how a tiny group of hiking sledder-surfers grew and developed into a driving force in America's increasingly pervasive mainstream youth culture. Or, just figure out what happened.

This is pretty subjective business, and since no one had written a history book, there were pitfalls. So many snowboarders, so little space and time. I tried to straddle the line between authenticity and accessibility. I wanted to give snow-boarders something to identify with, a book that they recognize, that doesn't distort and reduce snowboarding to caricature. Accessibility was harder.

Keeping an outsider's perspective became increasingly difficult as I learned more and spent more time on the snow. The two forces fought it out in my head for a year, my 25th, to be exact. I spent the '96–'97 winter combing contests, demos, trade shows, and industry shin-digs. After interviewing a few hundred people, this book is what I came up with. It is not exhaustive. It's does not address racing or non-US snowboarding. There are a hundred histories out there; this is only one.

Thanks for reading,

Susanna Howe

(s i c k)

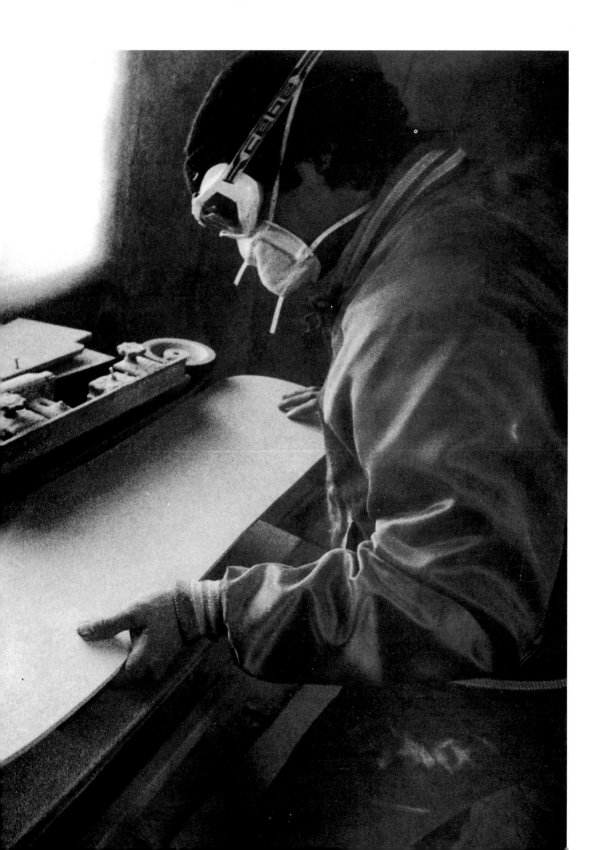

ONE EARLY HISTORY

WHERE DID SNOWBOARDING COME FROM?

EVERYONE LIKES TO TALK ABOUT THE "INVENTION," AS IF THERE WERE SOME KIND OF FAMILY TREE THAT ALL WENT BACK TO ONE PERSON, ONE "FOUNDER." IN TRYING TO TRACE THIS APOCRYPHAL GUY, I RAN INTO A HOTBED OF CONTROVERSY. SNOWBOARDING IS NEW ENOUGH THAT MANY OF THE EARLIEST PIONEERS ARE STILL AROUND, EACH CLAIMING OWNERSHIP OF THE OLDEST company. The truth is, no one person did it. People have been trying to stand up on their sleds forever, or at least as long as there have been sleds. But the surf fantasy of the '60s encouraged the entrepreneurial spirit of all kinds of inventors to take surfing's essence to different mediums. Snowboarding's earliest incarnations resulted from a logical conflation of sledding and surfing.

The earliest marketed snowboard came out in the height of surfing's popularity. It was called a Snurfer. The Snurfer brings us back to 1965 and a chemical gases engineer in Muskegon, Michigan named Sherman Poppen. One day Poppen was out behind his house, sledding with his daughters, when he saw something peculiar out of the corner of his eye. His 11-year-old daughter was sliding down the hill, standing up on her sled. Inspired, he ran back to his shop, bound two skis together, and tied a string to the nose that you could hold for stability. Poppen's wife called it a Snurfer and soon, all of his daughter's friends wanted one. In 1966, Sherman Poppen licensed the concept to Brunswick Bowling to manufacture Snurfers . . . and so, snowboarding was "born."

Between 1966 and 1977, Sherman Poppen sold over half a million Snurfers through grocery stores and sporting goods shops all over the country. With a retail price of $10-$30, they were not considered legitimate sports equipment. The Snurfer was a gimmick. "The Snurfer will become the Hula-Hoop of wintertime," boasted Poppen in the Muskegon Chronicle (Dec., 1966). But as it became more popular in the '70s, Poppen hosted Snurfer competitions at Blockhouse Hill in Muskegon. The contests attracted Snurfer enthusiasts from all over the country. One was Jake Burton Carpenter, a wannabe surfer from Long Island, who grew up to be the biggest snowboard manufacturer in the world.

Surf Fantasy

While rock and roll, the beat poets, and teenage identity emerged in the '50s, it wasn't until the early '60s that surfing joined the movement against the parent culture. The lure of surfing made California beaches the dream destination for a whole generation of leisure-seekers. Bruce Brown's surfing documentary, *The Endless Summer* (1964) captured the essence of the surf fantasy perfectly, complete with exotic travel, beautiful surf breaks, multicultural comedy, and the freewheelin' attitude that typified surf culture.

To Americans in the '60s, surfing represented Southern California, eternal childhood, freedom, quirkiness, remaining outside the mainstream or "square" scene, and above all, FUN. *The Endless Summer* was an unqualified smash hit, selling out even in Wichita, Kansas and grossing around 7 million dollars (it only cost 50 thousand to make). By the mid-'60s, surfing had it's own fashion and language, and even its own music and films. Although alternative at first, surfing punctured the mainstream with the Gidget movies *Beach Blanket Bingo* and *Ride the Wild Surf,* which took California beach style to mainstreet USA.

Surfing was far more than a sport; it was fast becoming big business. Even in its most mainstream incarnations, though, surfing embodied an entire philosophy for living, a lifestyle with which people could identify without actually riding the waves.

As surfers grew up, the lifestyle ceased to be limited to the young. Like '60s liberalism, the meaning of surfing evolved in the '70s. Yet it was the original surf fantasy that captured the imaginations of snowboarding's pioneers. Almost everyone was effected strongly by the surf fantasy in the beginning. Most of them came of age in the '60s, either longing for a surf board or riding on one. The surf fantasy spawned skateboarding and snowboarding, two cultures and industries that have grown out of and away from surfing, but have never separated themselves entirely. The board sport lifestyles now move together with the times, feeding one another, evolving and diversifying with the changing tastes of popular culture.

The poster image from *The Endless Summer* that evoked the dream of surfing.

Winterstick

A surfboard shaper named Dimitrije Milovich made perhaps the best snowboards of the 1970s. His early signature swallowtail fish designs even had metal edges, which although now standard, were virtually unheard of until the early '80s. Inspired by sliding on cafeteria trays while in college at Cornell University in Ithaca, New York, Milovich started making snowboards in 1969. His first usable board was two inches thick and five feet long. It was made out of redwood and had three deep steel skegs. It could only be turned by jumping on one end and then running over and jumping on the other. His designs were way ahead of their time primarily because he knew that although snowboarding is more akin to surfing, the snowboard itself had to function like a ski, with camber and sidecut.

Milovich moved from New York to Utah to start the company Winterstick in 1972. He disposed of the metal edges, as deep snow was, in his opinion, the only way to snowboard. Some of snowboarding's first national exposure was in articles on Winterstick in *Newsweek, Playboy,* and *Powder* magazines in 1975. At this point, Milovich sold boards in 11 foreign countries, but as snowboard design moved away from skegs and swallowtails, Milovich lost interest and left snowboarding in 1980. He got heavily involved in designing windsurfers and then started an engineering company, which he still runs today. Although he got out of the game before it really got started, his innovative designs have been copied heavily throughout snowboarding history and Milovich is recognized as a major pioneer of the sport.

The Making of an East Coast Mogul

"I don't remember the first time I rode a Snurfer," says Jake Burton, "but I do remember getting high at boarding school and running right into a tree with one. The loop was so small that you could only fit three fingers into it." Burton was only 14 in 1968 when he first tried Snurfing. "It was so clear that there was something there," he says. "Riding a Snurfer in powder isn't that different from riding a Supermodel or any of today's boards in powder. I mean it's different, but it's not *that* different. The sensation is the same."

Jake Burton grew up in Lawrence, New York, a wealthy beach community on Long Island. A child of the '60s and '70s, Burton was not immune to the surf fantasy. "I wanted a surf board so badly, and my parents never got me one. I always just had styrofoam boards and Boogie Boards, and you know that really makes you a second class citizen at the beach. The Snurfer thing was the same, but it was cool. It definitely had a cult thing. Not in a fanatical way, but we felt like we

were doing something cool that no one knew was so cool. It wasn't exploited by the mainstream. We weren't going out and doing it every day, but we were really into it."

Burton was more serious about skiing. A few years later, he was in college in Boulder, Colorado with long hair, a long beard, and a shot at the NCAA Champion ski team. But, after breaking his collarbone in a brutal car accident on the way to a Grateful Dead concert, his chances for the team were shot. Deflated, he left school and traveled around until his family summoned him home to New York to clean up his act. He enrolled as an economics major at New York University and got a part-time position assisting at a small mergers and acquisitions firm midtown. In May of 1977, Burton graduated from NYU and the investment firm took him on full time.

To his parents, Burton's life seemed to be happily back on track, but he was going crazy. "I kept thinking about Snurfers. I was surprised that no one had done anything with the idea," he recalls. "It seemed like a good way to make some dough," says Burton, "maybe even more than I was making." He quit his job and moved to Londonderry, Vermont to start Burton Boards. "I made classic mistakes, one after the other," admits Burton. He unrealistically thought that by starting in the middle of the winter, he'd make some cash—all he had to do was make 50 boards a day. He hired two relatives to run the company and quickly ran out of money. But he was working like a dog to make a good board, trying every material he could find at the hardware store: foam, fiberglass, steam-bent solid wood, and vertically laminated wood.

In 1978, Burton made 350 production boards out of laminated hardwood, not unlike a skateboard deck. "They cost $88," he recalls, "and everyone said it was too much." But Burton was trying to reach beyond the original Snurfer design, to make a board that was maneuverable and fast. He took one of his new blue boards to Poppen's Snurfer championships in '78 and caused a ruckus. Contest sponsors complained that Burton's board was not technically a Snurfer; it had a rubber water ski binding for the front foot. Other contestants argued that Burton should be allowed to compete, so they created an open category for non-Snurfer snurfers. Burton won.

The bindings were a major breakthrough and really marked the first difference between a Snurfer and a snowboard. A stationary front foot increased control and maneuverability. With stronger, lighter construction and bindings, Burton was modifying not just the board, but the action itself. Turns became easier and more stable. Burton's boards were leaving the comparatively primitive Snurfers in the dust. However, his boards still weighed 3 or 4 times what a snowboard weighs today, and with fins and no metal edges, camber, or P-tex, they were virtually unturnable in anything but very deep powder.

But so what? Burton loved powder and had no intention of taking his board to ski resorts; his Backhill boards were strictly for hiking up and riding ungroomed snow. "I thought it was going to be a sort of telemarking backcountry thing," he says, "for guys like me, in their 20s. I didn't realize then that kids would end up driving the sport. I should have realized that I got into Snurfing at 15. Why *wouldn't* kids like it?"

Public perception of the Snurfer was an obstacle. It had been marketed as a kids' toy for over ten years, and here was Burton trying to sell it to grownups. To stay afloat, Burton had to slim down his overhead, and bartend regularly. In the summers, he would return to Long Island where he could save money while teaching tennis. "One thing I learned," he says, "is that if you're starting a business, you have to be ready to lose some money, and operate on a small scale instead of trying to operate on a bigger scale in order to make money but then end up losing a lot more money. That's exactly what I did." Burton's crazy snow surfing vision didn't really fit into the mold of his urbane, upper-crust, New York upbringing. His friends and family made fun of his toy-making, asking him when he was going to stop the snowboard nonsense and get a real job. He cites their jeers and doubts as his main motivation during that time.

Although he had gotten into the business to make money, by the time he was broke, Burton's priorities had changed dramatically. He was a new man: "When I hit rock bottom, the whole deal was about 100,000 bucks over a couple of years. I realized that it was really important to me that the sport succeed. I stopped thinking of it as my company and started to just think of the sport. Shit. I just wanted that move to have been right. When I actually let go and started taking that attitude, that's when things really started to take off." Burton made a pledge to himself; he would always put the riding first. He started to take a longer range view. The sport was more important than an opportunity to make a quick buck. This was almost the opposite of Burton's initial attitude about starting a business. The pledge became a philosophy for Burton's company, and a model for the industry. Although its meaning was often lost in the flurry of media and big business, a reverence for the sport over business remained the crux of snowboarding's cherished value system.

Soon after Burton's splash at Blockhouse Hill, Poppen's manufacturers at Brunswick lost interest in Snurfers and unloaded the mismanaged company. Poppen decided to throw in the towel and go back to his chemical gases, and by

1979, this pioneer of snowboarding was out of the Snurfer business forever. The Snurfer's influence reverberated for many years. In the early '80s, every snowboard maker was either copying Milovich's Winterstick or Poppen's Snurfer. However, the Snurfer's commercial identity as a toy would be a handicap for snowboarding as it moved to the resorts. Even after the snowboard was legally declared a "directional ski device" in 1977 (which, unlike a sled, can be turned and controlled), its image as the Hula-Hoop of the '70s stuck well into the '80s.

Skate, Surf, Sims, Barfoot

Snowboarding's image is a descendent of the California surf and skate scene, and this in large part is due to '70s skateboard magnate Tom Sims. Sims grew up on the Jersey shore, less than 100 miles from Jake Burton, but the two could not have been more dissimilar; if Jake Burton is navy blue, Tom Sims is fire engine red. Sims' father had been an avid surfer in the '30s and as a kid Sims

Greg Weaver and Tom Sims, Tea Bowl, Santa Barbara, 1975.
PHOTO COURTESY TOM SIMS.

Sims factory team, 1977.
PHOTO RICK DAVIS,
COURTESY TOM SIMS.

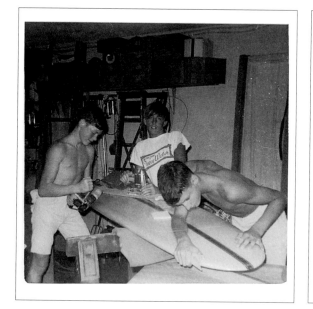

became obsessed with the California lifestyle. He lived for skateboarding from the time he saw one in Los Angeles at the age of 10. There were no skateboards in New Jersey, so Sims progressed somewhat in a vacuum. He spent all of his free time modifying his board, making up his own tricks, flying down bigger and bigger hills, and making boards in his garage for himself and his friends.

One day, Sims was sitting in his junior high shop class, bored. It was snowing outside and he was bummed that he wouldn't be able to skate after school. On a whim, he decided to make a skateboard for the snow. Materials were free, so he used a big, long piece of pine and glued carpet to the top for traction. A surfer at heart, Sims even waxed the base with his mom's good candles. When his creation still wouldn't move, he nailed some aluminum sheeting to the bottom. This, he claims, made all the difference in the world. Although his new kind of skateboard was fun, it was merely a substitute for surfing and skating in Sims' mind.

Sims' story about shop class predates any of his known boards by almost fifteen years. While Burton was trying out the Snurfer in 1968, Sims and his new friend Chuck Barfoot were trying to live the surf fantasy on the Jersey shore. Sick of the cold weather and flat ocean, the two finished high school and took off for Santa Barbara's prime surf breaks. They lived on a commune, grew their hair and tried to avoid being drafted. Sims spent his days modifying skateboards. He tried everything: as long surfboards were being replaced by shorter ones, Sims started making longer skateboards. To improve his surfing skills, he would skate on five-foot water skis with skateboard trucks mounted on them all the way down the Montecito hills above Santa Barbara. In 1971, his garage skateboard shop grew into a full-fledged company, and Barfoot, who had grown up working for his father's carpentry business, signed on as Sims' main constructor/craftsman.

Skateboarding blew up in California during the '70s, and Sims was at the forefront of innovation. Never afraid to think big, Tom Sims built a company that took skateboarding beyond anyone's expectations. With 38 employees and an in-house public relations department, Sims Skateboards developed a broad range of new skateboarding equipment and designs: new board shapes, such as the larger 10-inch "pig" boards, taperkick kicktails, routed-out channels, new wheel designs, glove designs, even bags and apparel. Equally groundbreaking was the cohesive visual identity in which all of these designs were packaged. The Sims image helped to shape the look of skateboarding and brought a higher production standard to the emerging culture.

Especially in the early days of his skateboard company, Sims' prowess and high media visibility as a competitive skater lent credibility to his business. Photos of Sims in the existing magazines, like *Skateboarder,* became iconographic: long hair, no shirt, no shoes, doing seemingly dangerous turns in illegal or at least exotic locations, all spoke of an individualistic attitude, in a sport slightly more

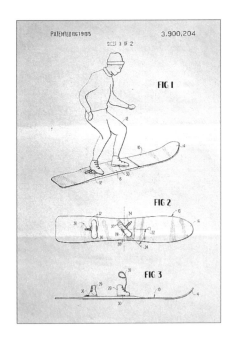

aggressive than surfing but incorporating its outsider status. The danger of pool riding and the attitude that went with it became central to skate culture, and in turn played a major part in Sims' development of snowboarding.

In 1977, an inventor from Maryland named Bob Weber approached Sims about making his patented "ski board" design a reality. This was at the height of Sims' success in the skateboard industry. He asked Barfoot to execute what would be called the Flying Yellow Banana. Skeptical, Barfoot put a Lonnie Toft pro model skateboard deck on a plastic shell with skegs. But after testing it out, Barfoot was bitten by the ski-boarding bug and got to work on improving the design. He quickly moved away from the banana design and with each successive design, he would go out to personally test each new board.

Barfoot vividly remembers his first test run on Christmas Day, 1978. He went to test his newest snowboard; it had signature flat ends with contours, but still no ski technology, no P-tex, no metal edges. Carrying a board that weighed over 15

Wee Willy Winkles and Lonnie Toft at Mammoth Mountain, California, testing the Flying Yellow Banana boards, 1978. PHOTOS COURTESY TOM SIMS.

pounds, he hiked up Entry 3 between Alta and Snowbird in Utah. It was kind of a secret spot, or so he thought. He laboriously walked up and up. Suddenly Barfoot heard something. He looked up to see someone coming down on a snowboard! "This was 1978!" Barfoot screams, "Snowboards didn't exist and here was a guy on a snowboard making short little turns, not long bottom carves like I did on my board. It turned out to be Jay Grell on a Snurfer. His brother Jeff Grell later invented high-back bindings." Chuck Barfoot was a surfer, so of course he made a board that would enable him to do long surfy bottom carves.

Chuck Barfoot on his first day, December 25, 1978. At Entry 3 between Snowbird and Alta in Utah. PHOTO COURTESY CHUCK BARFOOT.

The Grell brothers had a background in skiing, so their turns reflected the quicker, more aggressive attitude and techniques of skiing. These kinds of run-ins would become more and more common among the growing groups of snowboard innovators all over the western half of the country.

By the early 80's, America was sliding into a major recession and skateboarding, which had been booming through the late '70s, hit a serious slump. The pro contest series petered out and parks closed due to decreased attendance and high insurance liabilities. *Skateboarder* —the bible of park and pool skating—was replaced by a small rag from San Francisco called *Thrasher*. For the new punk scene of street skaters supported by *Thrasher,* it was just the beginning, but for big skate moguls like Sims, skating was as good as dead. By 1982, he had shifted his focus to snowboarding. In need of backing, Sims signed a skateboard and snowboard licensing deal with a larger, mainstream company called Vision

Chuck Barfoot, Fly Bowl, Montecito, California, 1985. PHOTO COURTESY CHUCK BARFOOT.

Sports. While it may have seemed like the solution to Sims' financial problems, it was a blow to many in the skate community. Some skaters embraced his venture into snowboarding, but others thought snowboarding was a joke and Sims a sellout. Even though snowboarding and skateboarding later cross-pollinated, the relationship between the hardcore skaters and snowboarding would remain tenuous.

Left out of the Vision deal, Barfoot struggled on by himself in a hut across the valley from where he lived with Bud Fawcett, another Sims employee who hadn't

Chuck Barfoot (middle) and Tom Sims (right),
testing boards in the Tahoe backcountry,
early '80s. PHOTO JAMES CASSIMUS, COURTESY TOM SIMS.

survived the deal. Fawcett would later become one of snowboarding's legendary
photographers. "Chuck wasn't a great business man, but he had some great
team riders," remembers Fawcett, "and they were all really faithful to him
because he was such a great guy." Barfoot woke at dawn to surf every morning
and worked construction during the day to make enough money to support his
snowboard-making habit at night. "We were standing in mud, working with elec-

trical tools and toxic chemicals all night," remembers Barfoot. "I was making 300 custom boards per year and selling them for $125 each. I was living on avocados." By 1985, Barfoot procured much needed backing and went from 300 to 3,500 boards, but he never stopped working seven days a week. Although Barfoot Snoboards never made the big dollars that Sims' or Burton's companies made, Barfoot deserves his legendary status as pioneer.

The '70s were quiet years for snowboarding, a part of history that belongs to the boardmakers themselves, who harnessed the laid back idealism of the '60s and the entrepreneurial spirit of the '70s to create a new industry. While skiing's glam freestyle scene was taking off with Suzy Chaffee (Chapstick) and Wayne Wong, people like Tom Sims, Jake Burton, Chuck Barfoot, Dimitrje Milovich, and others like the Grell brothers in Utah, the Derrah Brothers in Michigan, and Paul Graves were forging a more low-key, less fashion-oriented alternative. While all the early boardmakers had an alternative impulse in common, their plans for the sport varied. Burton's reserved but determined East Coast personality and ski racing background informed his vision for snowboarding in the early '80s, while the California lifestyle was at the core of Sims' plan. Having been immersed for over a decade in the volatile skateboard industry and its media-based structure, Sims, with all the right media contacts, was poised to build a personality-driven hero-worship machine of promotion for snowboarding. As the competitive arena opened up in the '80s, the two would start to butt heads regularly, but ultimately, the Sims-Burton, East-West coast rivalry would prove healthy for snowboarding's advancement.

I remember we'd get on the bus in Utica, New York to go to the ski hill, wearing wetsuits. We were wearing wetsuits, carrying snowboards, middle of winter on public transport. We felt totally stupid. I think people thought it was Halloween or something.

—Trevor Graves, photographer

We'd get so much flack. Baker was full of serious skiers and they'd yell at us, "Hey, the ocean's that way!" or "Get a boat to tow that thing" "Some day you'll be able to afford two!" All these little jabs. But as we got better and the equipment got better, it went from people heckling us to people being impressed and cheering us on.

—Jeff Fulton, pro

[Mike] Olson was a freak. He used to show up at events with plaid Bermuda shorts, a cutoff t-shirt and his board was called, "No Guarantees," which he markered on there. We were all tech with our parachute pants, Sims had white speed suits, but Gnu was all graffiti.

—Chris Sanders, CEO, Avalanche Snowboards

In Colorado, the first snowboarders weren't really mountain men. They were more sort of sporto, pot-smoking skiers. Tim Windell, Dave Dowd, and Kevin Delaney lured everyone into it. We used to go up to Loveland Pass during full moon. You could see sparks from people's boards hitting rocks.

—Troy Bush, CEO, Twist/Tuesday/Titan Snowboard Clothing

People from the East Coast were totally over stoked. They're just so full of intensity about what they're doing, while the California guys were a lot more mellow about it, or at least that's what they acted like.

—Jason Ford, pro

Out here [in SoCal] it's Hollywood, for sure. But that's snowboarding. Even Colorado and Utah are kind of Hollywood. But back East, everyone's a bro. They're all good ole boys. The east coast has always breeded sick snowboarders and they don't get known. Out here, a lot of mediocre riders get sponsored, just 'cause they know some bro.

—Jeff Brushie, pro

TWO POCKETS

TWO EARLY HUBS OF RIDING

WHILE THE '70S BELONGED TO SNOW-
BOARDING'S PIONEER PRODUCERS, THE
EARLY '80S BROUGHT A NEW GENERA-
TION OF RIDERS TO THE MOUNTAINS:
THE CONSUMERS. SNOWBOARDS WERE
BECOMING AVAILABLE AT SKI SHOPS,
AND FROM THERE, SMALL NETWORKS
OF RIDERS EMERGED IN WASHINGTON,
CALIFORNIA, UTAH, COLORADO, AND
VERMONT. WITH NO MEDIA TO SHOW
WHAT OTHER SNOWBOARDERS WERE

Andy Coghlan, pro racer, Stratton, Vermont, 1982.
PHOTO HUBERT SCHRIEBL, COURTESY JAKE BURTON.

Mike Olson and Jon Heine, Seattle, Washington, 1980. They later co-founded Gnu.
PHOTO COURTESY MIKE OLSON.

like, each group of backcountry hikers had its own version of snowboarding, shaped by local climate and terrain, equipment, and roots (eg., skiing, skateboarding, BMX biking, mountaineering, and surfing). It was a highly experimental time, and early '80s boards were all different shapes, with all different features: rocker, multiple fins, swallow tails, fish tails, and all different kinds of sidecut.

Commercial boards around this time were mainly Burtons and Wintersticks, although emerging companies like Gnu in Washington and Avalanche in Lake Tahoe, California had strong local followings. Lake Tahoe, a ritzy ski resort at the foot of the Sierra Nevada mountains, was one of the first and most active snowboarding spots. Twenty-three miles long and six thousand feet above sea level, the lake went through a boom when nearby Squaw Valley hosted the 1960 Winter Olympics. With the glamour of the Olympics and more accommodations, Tahoe became a trendy destination ski resort. It wasn't the fancy vacationers who started snowboarding in Tahoe, though. Instead, it started with a few local kids.

The first snowboarders in Lake Tahoe were a couple of North Shore high school freshmen. In 1978, 15-year-old Bob Klein saw an ad in *Powder Magazine* for Winterstick and couldn't take his eyes off of it. As a skateboarder and a skier, he was dying to try out a snowboard, and he convinced his dad to call and get some boards. Winterstick sent them two boards, saying that if they could get them on the lifts at a Lake Tahoe resort, they could keep the boards. "I was stoked," remembers Klein, "because I lived at the foot of Tahoe Ski Bowl and I knew the guys who ran it, so it was no trouble getting up the lifts." Winterstick also sent Klein a 16 mm instructional film, filled with shots of beautiful Utah powder turns. Klein took it to school and showed it to his high school history class. In that class was a veritable who's who of legendary Lake Tahoe snowboarders; Terry Kidwell, Allen Arnbrister, and Tom Burt were all students.

Kidwell, Arnbrister, and Klein saw snowboarding as a way to skate on snow. They set up a gully near the dump as a sort of skate ramp, and when the snow dumped they practiced every day after school. It took three or four hours to make the jump rideable, but then they could do skate tricks off of it on their snowboards. By 1982, word had reached Tom Sims in Santa Barbara that there was a group of snowboarders who rode a natural half-pipe of snow in Lake Tahoe. A half-pipe, usually made out of wood or concrete for skateboards, was unheard of at this point in snowboarding. "One day, Tom Sims showed up with a bunch of punk skaters," remembers Klein. "It kind of sucked, actually, because they all acted so important and kind of took over our spot, acting all punk and throwing cigarette butts around." Once a week or so, some skaters would show up with a photographer. "There were two groups at the Tahoe City half-hipe," recalls Klein. "First, me and my friends from high school. Locals. Then the skater media people. We would build up the wall all day and then they would come and ruin it. It was cool though. [Pro skater] Steve Caballero was there."

The TC Half-Pipe was just what Tom Sims was looking for. He had been trying to get his team skaters into snowboarding, but was having some trouble. "The day *Thrasher* magazine came out in '79, skating and surfing ceased to have a connection," declares Sims. "Skaters hated surfers. Skaters hated everyone. 'Everything sucks.' was the punk mantra that *Thrasher* espoused and that was modern skate culture in 1982." This was the attitude that was brought to snowboarding by Sims' skaters. The Tahoe City Half-Pipe was the first hotbed for skate-influenced snowboarding, a first mecca for "freestyle" snowboarders.

As this new style of riding gained momentum, Terry Kidwell emerged as the undisputed leader. "You can really trace the whole freestyle thing to one guy," says Jake Burton. "Terry's the man." He has been remembered as the father of freestyle. Says Kidwell of the title: "I guess people remember it that way because I won a lot of contests. If Allen Arnbrister hadn't gotten into trouble with certain [drugs] and gone to jail, he probably would have had my career. We were just trying to simulate skateboarding on snow instead of surfing or skiing. I

Terry Kidwell,
Donner Summit,
1986. PHOTO
BUD FAWCETT.

guess that was a little different at the time." Kidwell was picked up by Sims almost immediately in '82 and went on to inspire a great legacy of freestyle riders.

Avalanche

Down on the south shore of Lake Tahoe, there was a different type of riding going on. Inspired by Poppen's Snurfer, an avid skier named Chris Sanders started making boards out of his South Lake garage in the early '80s. Every weekend, Sanders and his girlfriend Bev hiked up at Lake Tahoe's Soda Springs to ride his homemade boards, and every weekend Bev would end up selling them to some curious skiers. This semi-business went on for a while, until he and Bev got married and started Avalanche Snowboards in 1982. The Avalanche crew was made up of Chris and Bev's friends, mostly skiers who wanted to try something new. "Skiing was so elitist in the early '80s," says Chris, "really cliquey, exclusive. It was so dependent on the cool factor. Bev was in the right

clique but she explained to me how lame skiing was. When we were starting up snowboarding, it was incredibly inclusive." The Avalanche crew was formed by amazing skiers who wanted to break out of the scene. They liked snowboarding because it was style-oriented whereas skiing had an indisputable standardized technique. As skiers, the Avalanche crew were looking for new ways to challenge themselves on the mountain. They were older and quite different from the half-pipe clan. Bonnie Leary, Jim Zellers, and Klein's friend, Tom Burt, were the adventurous types, always looking for new peaks to descend and new ways to descend them.

Olson and the Northwest

The pioneer often credited with the development of the modern carving snowboard is Mike Olson, a goofy genius from Seattle. When his mom wouldn't buy him a skateboard in 1977, this 12-year-old made his own. "I had one Sims board, but I made most of them myself," reports Olson. "I remember sitting in our back-yard drawing a sketch for a skateboard and dreaming about surfing. I remember suddenly looking down thinking how great it would be if I could make a huge skateboard/surf board/ski thing out of the picnic table bench. That's what really got me thinking about snowboards." Olson made his first board in his 7th grade shop class, and kept making them through high school.

But in 1983, Olson dropped out of college to start Gnu Snowboards. "I was studying math," he recalls, "and my friends were pissed that I didn't have time to build boards for them. I thought I'd get it out of my system in five years, max." Olson never really thought Gnu would go anywhere. "In the early and mid-'80s, even skateboarding was in a real down phase. I had a lot of friends who were still skaters and I couldn't even get them to try snowboarding. They had no inter-est in going to the mountains." Olson's goals were never on the scale of Sims' or Burton's. He wasn't charging forward to father the sport of the future. Olson wanted to make enough boards for himself, his friends, and enough other peo-ple to pay his way.

Olson's Northwestern upbringing taught him to enjoy the simple things. He came from a family of fishermen and teachers, except for his dad, who was one of the original Sun Valley ski bums. "He used to side slip the trails all morning for a free pass every afternoon," Olson claims, proud of his father's lifestyle choice. "He was really proud of never skiing on new skis. He knew this guy who worked at the dump near K2 on Vashon Island, who would call us when he had a pair of salvageable skis. My dad and I would rebuild them together." By the time he got to making snowboards, Olson had an intimate relationship with ski construction. He also shaped windsurfers and surf boards. "My family never had money. We learned to operate on no money, so money wasn't really the goal. The goal was just fun. I was 19 years old." But Olson's rich alpine and board sports background set him up to contribute heavily to the development of snowboarding, both equipment-wise and with his unique way of marketing and doing business.

Dan Donnelly,
Northwest
native and
MBHC member,
Soda Springs,
California, 1985.
PHOTO BUD FAWCETT.

The Northwest is known most for its steep terrain, varied snow conditions, and unforgiving weather patterns. Unlike Tahoe, where the sun shines 300 days per year, Mt. Baker, situated three hours from Seattle on the Canadian border, is usually cloudy and dark. Unlike Colorado, where it usually snows at night, Northern Washington's storms roll into Mt. Baker at about four or five in the morning and taper off at around four in the afternoon. These are the elements that formed not only the physical conditions of the Northwest, but the personalities of its riders as well. To brave the elements in the Northwest, a person has to be committed to a vision. A group of just such individuals was snowboarding up at Mt. Baker in the early '80s.

MBHC

Nineteen-year-old Jeff Fulton was managing a bicycle motorcross (BMX) team for his dad's bike shop in Mt. Vernon, Washington in 1979. He met a guy named Bob Barci, another bike/skate shop owner from the Seattle area, who was just getting into selling Snurfers and Burton Boards. Barci lent a board to Fulton and after the first day, Fulton was the proud owner of a brand new Burton Backhill. "There were two little guys on the BMX team named Craig Kelly and Dan Donnelly," remembers Fulton. "I tried to get them to buy boards too, but no one wanted to shell out 90 bucks, so I talked my dad into having a few snowboards in the shop to rent out. I convinced him that they would pay for themselves in no time. I just wanted to have some boards around for my friends to ride." Kelly, Donnelly, Fulton, and another friend, Eric Swanson were the first people to ride at Mt. Baker. Within a few years, they were all pros, and Kelly was the world champion.

The harshness of the northwestern weather never stopped the Northwest crew. "I remember riding under chair[lift]s four and five one day," describes Fulton. "It's pretty steep there, but the icy wind was blowing so hard it was actually hard to get down. We were yelling into the wind and I was thinking, 'God! You have to

Bud Fawcett's first snowboarding trip, here at Park West, Utah. Afterward, they would go on to Jackson Hole, Wyoming and Mt. Baker, Washington for the first Banked Slalom Race. Kidwell is fourth from left and Klein is sixth from left. PHOTO BUD FAWCETT.

be totally hardcore to be out here.' From then on I started writing MBHC on my board, standing for Mount Baker Hard Core." Before long, the lifties at the mountain and Fulton's buddies Eric Janko, Carter Turk, Craig Kelly, and Dan Donnelly were all down with the MBHC. "Snowboarding was easily the most important thing in all of our lives," concludes Fulton. Not only were these riders the renegades on the mountain because they were snowboarding, they were the renegades of the country because they were dealing with the roughest conditions and terrain in total anonymity. They took extreme pride in their status as unsung outsiders.

Mt. Baker and Lake Tahoe have always produced great snowboarders. Of course pockets in Colorado, Utah, or Vermont have their own conditions and stories about the earliest snowboarders—like the story of Myron Knappshaffer, an old man who lived atop Colorado's Berthoud Pass, who pounded cracked steel edges onto all the local riders' boards before anyone manufactured boards with edges. There are as many stories as there are mountains, but the one theme that

Burton crew. PHOTO COURTESY JAKE BURTON.

united all riders in the early years was snowboarding's open-ended identity. There was an inclusive, community spirit pervading the sport, a fun, nonjudgmental scene that valued personal style. Unlike skiing, snowboarding at this point wasn't about money or status or popularity or "doing it right." It didn't help your image at school, because it had none itself, but to other snowboarders, riding a snowboard qualified you as an immediate friend.

Nobody really wanted us at the resorts. Why would they? The behavior thing was huge. I mean, I ride on closed trails and do all of that but these kids were doing stupid stuff on purpose. It was cool to do stupid stuff. So we had to be like cops. When Stratton's resort manager, Paul Johnson let us on the lifts at Stratton, he said that we had to police it ourselves, so we had this screwy certification program. Mark Heingartner would check out how people rode and give them stickers, upper mountain certification or just lower mountain certification. . . . It was like a goddamn police state. It sucked, but it was all for a reason. We later got all this shit for it from the magazines, like we were nazis or something. You know, you just can't win.

—Jake Burton, Founder and President, Burton Snowboards

THREE RESORT ACCEPTANCE

OUT OF THE WOODS

GETTING SNOWBOARDING ACCEPTED AT SKI AREAS WAS THE SINGLE MOST IMPORTANT CONTRIBUTION TO ITS GROWTH IN THE '80S. "AT THAT TIME, SNOWBOARDING WAS A REAL CAUSE," SAYS BEV SANDERS. "I WAS TOTALLY DEDICATED BECAUSE I WAS NOT INTO HIKING." THE SNOWBOARDING DEMO-GRAPHIC CHANGED AS RESORTS OPENED, FROM THE MOUNTAINEER

and crossover skier type, to a whole new young and aggressive snowboarder, a stranger to both the resort and the backcountry. "At the very beginning, skiers didn't mind," says Bev. "They thought it was novel, as long as there weren't very many of us. We were undercover, on our best behavior, and we dressed like skiers to seem legitimate." Then it all changed. "As soon as there were new kids who didn't realize how tenuous our position was, there was attitude. I tried to reason with the ski resort managers." Bev was a good spokesperson because she was a woman and over 21 years old. As one of the first women to embrace snowboarding, and a great skier, she helped public perception immeasurably.

Bev and Chris Sanders ran The Slide Safety Certification Program, which was not unlike the Burton test at Stratton: "We asked kids if they were planning on using foul language or ducking lift lines," remembers Bev. "Then we'd give them a little test to make sure they could turn and stop. It seems ridiculous, I know. But it was the only way to get on the mountain, and I would have done anything at that point." The program was mostly an opportunity for the Sanderses to say "Don't act like a jerk and mess this up for the rest of us!" However, it created a flurry of liability problems and didn't last long.

Bad behavior aside, snowboarders hardly ever ride down the fall line the way skiers do. While skiers tend to cut a straight line of aggressive turns, snow-boarders—especially the ones with surf and skate backgrounds—tend to weave and cut across trails and duck in and out of the trees. And they love powder. Skiers quickly grew annoyed by the lack of symmetry and unpredictability of the snowboarders. Even after the collective ability level of snowboarders rose, skiers were angered by the powder-hogging lines that snowboarders chose.

In the end, money talked. Skiing was in a down cycle. The '70s had been a major boom period for skiing, but after the freestyle ski craze died down and the Mahre brothers were no longer Olympic champions, skiing was losing money. Resorts were closing all over the country. Soon, snowboarders represented too many dollars for resort managers to turn them away. Small, poor ski areas gave snowboarding its first chance, but soon, larger destination resorts were recharged with the young energy of snowboarding's consumer base. But, skiers continued to have a hard time sharing the mountain. Skier-snowboarder contro-versy mounted throughout the '80s.

FOUR THE FIRST CONTESTS

THE COLD WAR

TOM SIMS REPORTS THAT AT THE EARLI-
EST SNOWBOARDING RACES, THERE
WERE NO GATE ATTENDANTS, SO THE
GATES WOULD FALL AND STAY DOWN
AND THE WINNER WOULD BE THE GUY
WITH THE FEWEST GATES TO DEAL WITH.
EVERYONE WAS DRUNK AND DISORDER-
LY, AND REALLY JUST THERE TO REVEL IN
THE RARITY OF AN OCCASION THAT
MADE SNOWBOARDING SEEM LIKE A
REAL CULTURE WITH MORE THAN

At the first Nationals in Vermont, 1983 Burton (left) and Sims (right) in wetsuit. PHOTOS HUBERT SCHRIEBL, COURTESY JAKE BURTON.

two or three members. Contests galvanized snowboarders into a larger, national community. Jake Burton and Tom Sims hosted the two major annual contests in the early '80s. Each was coming from a cultural position rooted in his environment, one in New England, the other in California. The two pioneers had very different visions for this new sport. The Burton contest led the way in '83, followed by the Sims contest in '84, and another kind of contest altogether in the Northwest in '85.

S u s a n n a   H o w e

East

"Tom rode, I rode, everybody rode back then," says Jake Burton of the first National Snowboarding Championships at Snow Valley, Vermont. "It wasn't even just my team and Tom's team either. There were the Flite guys from Rhode Island and the Winterstick guys from Utah, the Barfoot guys, the Colorado contingent, the Michigan guys, the Vermont guys, and the Tahoe people." Burton brought his newest boards to the first Nationals in '83: the Performer and the Powergun.

Tom Hsieh: My skater friends and I went to the '85 World Championships in Soda Springs. Tom Sims was running the show. At the awards banquet, there was this huge fight between him and Ken Achenbach. Someone owed someone money and Ken had won a prize for the half-pipe and Tom was giving out the checks and he held a check out for Ken and then pulled it away, saying, "But you owe me money," right in front of 400 people. They started yelling at each other, really going at it. I was just sitting there thinking, "Wow. This would make great copy." I launched the magazine a year later. It lasted until '91.

Were you into skate mags at the time?

TH: Oh yeah. *Thrasher* was the bible. I read it cover to cover every month. I was very influenced by that magazine. They really reported the culture as it was. *ISM* was pretty much after the *Thrasher* model. I didn't really know other magazines at that point. There was a lot of struggle between Burton and Sims. Jake's whole thing at the time was that the sport needed credibility and professionalism. He hated the whole thrash, "skate and destroy" attitude. Sims was all, "Hey this is my roots," skating, half-pipes, vertical. That early conflict was great for me as a publisher.

I was in the middle of these two guys, the devil on one shoulder and the angel on the other. I would get calls at three in the morning from those guys. Jake would call up and say that I had too many guys in the air, not enough guys on the ground. That basically meant that I had too many Sims (freestyle) riders and not enough Burton (alpine) riders. I couldn't believe I was hearing this.

MARCH 1985   75 CENTS

ABSOLUTELY RADICAL

SNOWBOARD MAGAZINE

VOL. 1 NO. 1

Rider Keith Kimmel on the first cover of Tom Hsieh's magazine (he switched the name to ISM after the first issue).

Both models had heelstraps, which kept both feet completely attached to the board, as opposed to the earlier models that covered only the front of the foot, like a slip-on sandal. The Burton team was nervous about being strapped to the board, but they rose to the occasion and swept most of the events.

Contests gave snowboarding a center, a sense of legitimacy. "Sims and Burton were both doing this factory-manufactured team thing starting around then," says Burton. "We were fighting for our lives commercially. The mentality was very different, not so individualistic as it is now. It was a totally alpine deal. We all had our speed suits that had our names on them." Team allegiance was strong; being on the winning team was almost as important as winning the contest. People would stand at the edge of the course and yell, "Go Burton!" or "Go Sims!" rather than rooting for specific riders, as they do today.

Burton's main team riders in the earliest days were coming from a ski racing background. "[Andy] Coghlan and those guys had been spat out of the ski scene for political reasons. A lot of our early riders were ski racers, but they just didn't fit into the very disciplined, structured, pro-racer mold. If you pissed off one coach, you were screwed forever, and I guess that's what most of our early riders did. They were wild cards in skiing, and snowboarding was much less hardcore than skiing." Although snowboarding offered a place for skiing misfits, the racing team mentality was being imposed on a sport that until now consisted of friends hiking in the backcountry and finding the best way down the mountain. Competition, especially racing, was a huge step toward a more commercially packaged period for snowboarding.

West

Tom Sims had very different ideas about snowboarding: "On the East Coast, you had your Andy Coghlans and Chris Karols, typical New England guys who would have been ski racers," says Sims. "In California, only skaters were really snow-

**Allen Arnbrister, early
half-pipe legend, Soda
Springs, California, 1984.**
PHOTO BUD FAWCETT.

**Burton team at World
Championships,
Soda Springs, 1985.**
PHOTO COURTESY JAKE BURTON.

boarding. There was definitely a clash of cultures. Ours was a California skate scene and theirs was a conservative CB jacket culture." The spring following the Nationals, Sims hosted the World Snowboarding Championships at Soda Springs, California. He was the father of snowboarding on the West Coast. Says Bob Klein of Sims' bravado: "That contest was all about Sims. I got to the mountain and everyone was waiting for Sims to let people on the lifts. He went up with his team first. He made turns down the freshly groomed race course and his team riders followed him, placing gates where he made his turns. That's how they set the course." For the Sims team, mostly skaters, this course-setting method seemed normal enough. For anyone coming from a ski racing background, the entire Burton team included, it seemed ridiculous.

Sims' big surprise was the carefully molded half-pipe that he had built for the contest, a replica of the Tahoe City Half-Pipe, where he and his team had been practicing. Introducing this new event, Sims was trying to drive the focus away from racing into a whole new direction: freestyle snowboarding.

Ironically, Burton, who made waves with his innovations at Poppen's Snurfer contest in '78, considered Sims' half-pipe alien to the sport that he was trying to legitimize. An argument ensued. Was snowboarding history being made, or was the half-pipe a joke? This brought the issue of snowboarding's identity straight to the fore. Who could say what was legitimate? Skateboarding itself had once been laughed at, but had grown into a multimillion-dollar industry with an inter-

The Modern Snowboard

Contests threw progression into hyperspeed. Riders were pushed to go faster and jump higher. Boardmakers were more aware than ever that there was a future in making snowboards, and more inspired than ever by their inventive colleagues. All at once in the middle of the '80s, the most progressive manufacturers realized that ski technology was appropriate and necessary for the modern snowboard. Metal edges, P-tex, camber, and sidecut found their way into snowboard construction, mainly in the shops of Mike Olson in Seattle, Chris Sanders in Lake Tahoe, and Jake Burton in Vermont. By 1986, all three were making boards in Austria, capitalizing on its advanced ski engineering, rich alpine heritage, open-minded attitude, and a favorable exchange rate. Even though alpine and freestyle snowboarding were starting to grow apart, snowboarding culture was becoming more cohesive. Most importantly, each equipment advance made snowboarding easier to learn, which drew in new riders. The growth in numbers would result in a more coherent and identifiable snowboarding culture.

Gnu's Mike Olson was the first to use aggressive sidecut and market his snowboards as carving machines. Olson: "I was up at Stevens Pass skiing and I broke a ski, so I was trying to ski on one ski by putting my free foot behind the other, in a sort of surf stance. It was carving really well and a light bulb went off in my head. I went home

thinking about radical sidecut." Shifting the emphasis from a passive, surf stance and movement, to a more ski-related, aggressive forward charging posture, Olson was pioneering the second phase of snowboard engineering. To make the movement away from surfing complete, Olson finally ripped off the plastic fins, which had acted like a break on hard pack snow.

Back in Vermont, Burton team riders like Andy Coghlan were complaining that they needed more control on the rock-hard Vermont slopes. The boards had metal edges, but, as Burton says, "We were doing it all ass backwards, starting with a wooden board and routing out space to put in metal." Later, most boards would have light, thin, wooden cores with plastic and metal attached.

Burton went on a ski holiday in Austria with his girlfriend Donna's family in 1982 and met with ski manufacturers: "I went to see this one guy who was making this thing called a Swingbo. It was like a skateboard deck with these sort of loop bindings on top of two very short skis that had incredible sidecut. It carved really well. It turned out we had a conflict of interest and he couldn't manufacture boards for me, but he sent me to see this manufacturer called Keil about two hours away in Salzburg. I got there at like 11:30 at night and the guy's daughter did the translating. We negotiated all night and made a deal. His father had made wagons, he was making x-country skis, and then at some point he went full time making snowboards for us." In 1985, with his new wife, Donna, Burton moved to Austria and started Burton USA's Austrian counterpart in Innsbruck, Burton Sportartikel.

Also in 1985, Avalanche's Chris Sanders introduced a new kind of board, with camber and sidecut, and the first plate bindings to be worn with hard, plastic boots. The system provided more energy and control. "Our first ski-board launched everybody out of their garages, where snowboards were being built like skateboards," says Sanders. "We built this whole new mold at Palé. Bev and I had to bankroll all of our money into this new board and if it didn't work, we were gonna be screwed." Sanders nervously gave the new board to his team rider Tom Burt to try out with the hard boots and plate bindings. "I could have never made that board work so well," continues Sanders, "but thank God, Tom just zooted down the hill, making perfect turns. In my eyes, Tom proved that ski technology belonged in snowboarding.

"Then everything went horribly wrong. None of us were really into racing. We were into freeriding. But the Europeans came out with a step-in hard boot system, so then everyone associated my system with Europeans and racing and ski-

ing, which was totally uncool at the time. About five Americans wanted to look like that. It was a marketing disaster for us. The popular thing was to be different, American, the opposite of skiing." Europeans came out with hard boot systems at a culturally defining moment for snowboarding, and no one would be able to associate hard boots or step-in bindings with freeriding for another decade. Avalanche riders, like Tom Burt, Damian Sanders, and Jim Zellers freerode in the uniplate system for years, but they were the only ones. The marketing arena at the time was too strongly dominated by the soft boot and highback binding combination.

As alpine and freestyle disciplines began to demand different things from equipment, freestyle boards emerged from the shops of Sims and Barfoot. The first freestyle board from Sims was also the first signature pro model, designed to meet the needs of "the father of freestyle," Terry Kidwell. Chuck Barfoot's "twin-tip" board in 1987 was designed by his team riders from Canada, Ken Achenbach and Neil Daffern. It offered a wider stance and two identical ends for forward/backward riding. The twin-tip innovation revolutionized pipe riding and riding "fakie" became integral to every snowboarder's personal progression.

national contest circuit of its own. But this was snowboarding, and the East Coast team saw the half-pipe as a rip off of skateboarding and a cheap way for the Sims team to win. Burton adamantly protested its inclusion in the contest.

To this day, many West Coasters say that Burton was just pissed that his team would lose a freestyle event, and that he wanted snowboarding to be just like ski racing. Many New Englanders say that Sims was an egomaniac with a grand marketing scheme to get all skateboarders to embrace his version of snowboarding and make a trillion dollars. Either way, snowboarding's future direction and the industry's marketing position were being fought over by two very determined, opinionated personalities.

Baker Banked Slalom

The Northwest snowboard scene managed to stay out of the snowboarding identity controversy. In 1985, a small group of shop owners led by a man named Bob Barci decided to have a different type of snowboard race up at Mt. Baker. Barci was friends with all the BMX, skater, and snowboarder kids in the area, and knew that while they were into speed, they were also into riding the natural gullies of Mt. Baker. "Tom Sims used to have this thing called the Sims Challenge, where if you beat him, he would give you a snowboard," remembers Barci. "When we decided we wanted to have the race on the walls of Chute #1, I called up Sims and he agreed to come up and do the Sims Challenge at Baker." Barci set up a race course on one of Baker's long, half-pipe-shaped gullies; the gates were placed up on its walls, so that to ride through the course, you had to pump around the gates as though skateboarding on a ramp.

Snowboarders road-tripped from all over the country to compete in this curious contest. Anyone who beat Tom Sims would get a Sims Snowboard. No one did, but everyone had a great time and saw the best snowboarders in the world. The Banked Slalom became an annual legendary event and it's low-key vibe continued throughout the years of hype and commercialism.

Mike Olson at first Mt. Baker Banked Slalom, 1985. PHOTO BUD FAWCETT.

The Baker Race gave locals a chance to get in on the ground floor. In 1986, one of the original MBHCs, Craig Kelly emerged from obscurity and came in third, right behind Tahoe superstars Terry Kidwell and Shaun Palmer. That same year, Rob Morrow came in fourth: "I remember the awards ceremony, when this guy from Sims yelled to me from the balcony, 'Hey Rob, give me a call on Monday.' I was freaking out," says Morrow. "His words were echoing in my head." Morrow and Kelly were picked up by Sims; Kelly went on to win the world champion title and Morrow, junior world champion. While it was an important race for the industry, the Baker Banked Slalom always brought the meaning of snowboarding competition back to its purest, least commercialized form. Attitude was not allowed.

Snowboarding in the '80s became progressively more focused on competition. As the companies grew, they set up more organized teams that would travel together as a force. Contests were a place where the media and team scouts

At first Mt. Baker Banked Slalom. From left, Terry Kidwell, Bob Klein, and Tom Sims.
PHOTO BUD FAWCETT.

would look for new talent—the only outlet through which riders could show their prowess. They were also the only opportunity for everyone to meet and check out new equipment, riding styles, and fashions. Competitions were cultural hotbeds in the '80s, where a relatively stratified scene came together and percolated. Later, the media would replace competition as the means to make a career, but for snowboarders in the '80s, contests were the only way to be a pro.

Sponsors quickly learned all they had to do was dress us up in Day-Glo and catch somebody on camera saying, 'Gnarly air, dude,' and they were guaranteed 15 seconds on the evening news. We all knew that the sponsors and the media had no idea what the sport was about, but if dressing up like clowns and posing for MTV meant a few days of freeriding, most of us were in.

—David Alden, *Snowboarder Magazine* Evolution Issue, October '95

'87 Worlds at Breck . . . ABC was putting it on TV . . . Damian ended up calling Paul Alden a fag and I had to make him apologize. There ended up being this huge crazy snowball fight when they announced the results, and this Swatch guy came up to me, right to my face and screamed, "You're ruining everything!" So I stood on a chair and screamed to the crowd, "If any of you thought you had a chance at this contest, you were wrong. You didn't because of this man right here." At the awards ceremony, Bev and I were sitting there all alone at a big table because none of the team riders would come. Then they walk in with like 15 friends, all dressed from head to toe in black. Paul Alden looked so scared and was pulling security guys aside saying that there was going to be trouble at our table.

—Chris Sanders, CEO, Avalanche Snowboards

I met Jeff Brushie in '87 at Loon mountain. Andy Coghlan introduced me to Brush and said "He's gonna go places. He rides like Terry Kidwell." I looked at Jeff and he was all shy and quiet, with this crusty, boogered-up nose, and he was racing on a freestyle board with a swallowtail. He had this really low style, and he pumped around turns, a lot like Craig Kelly back then. That next weekend we ended up going to Nashoba Valley and it was the first half-pipe contest. Todd Richards was there, wearing full skate gear, helmet, kneepads, the whole nine. The pipe was just a taco, really shitty but Brush showed up with his loped-off Depeche Mode haircut and his Ratbones skate jacket with the Powell logos on it. He just busted HUGE method airs at the bottom of the pipe and everyone was so stoked. He was an icon for sure.

—Trevor Graves, photographer

There was a PSTA tour that Body Glove was sponsoring, and Palmer hit the main sponsor guy from Body Glove with a hot dog. The guy was all calm, going "Oh yeah, we've done surf tours. We know how to deal with these people." They pulled out after that. Culturally, none of the riders were prepared to deal with contest structure, and financially it wasn't worth it.

—Jeff Galbraith, Senior Editor, *Snowboarder Magazine*

Breck in '86 was weird. People were leaning over the pipe and almost getting hit in the face. Terry Kidwell did a handplant and his board got hung up on a person who was watching. Craig Kelly, Mike Ranquet, and I went out to Breck for the Worlds in '86 together. We borrowed Mike's mom's VW van to go. Ranquet was still too young to drive, but his mom let us drive it. Mike goes to the store and buys watercolors and paints all over the van. Metallica, Santa Cruz, all over the van. He thought it was going to wash off but it never did, even in rainstorms. We finally get to Colorado and the van is all messed up; we had to push start it everywhere we went. On the way home it finally totally died outside of Oregon and Mike's mom had to come pick us up.

—Jeff Fulton, pro

Snowboarding was for gay, lame, neon dorks then. I was one of them.

—Lee Crane, Editor, *Snowboarding Online*

At the Breck Worlds one time, Dana Nicholson comes to the bottom of the hill, probably in about 37th place. Bev had taught him to react like he won: arms up, go to your knees and claim victory. He did this really well, and MTV totally fell for it. The winner never got a thing. Dana got an entire spot on MTV, describing the snow-boarder's breakfast, which was Cocoa Puffs with Pop Rocks sprinkled on top and Jolt cola. Pop Rocks and soda were punk in those days 'cause that kid had died from the combo. It was flirting with the devil. Dana was a great interview. Always had a girl on his arm. Very media ready.

—Chris Sanders, CEO, Avalanche Snowboards

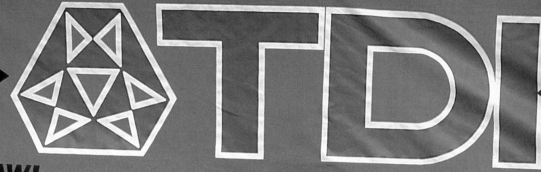

Shaun Palmer prevails at the peak of competition, 1990 Breckenridge World Championships. Craig Kelly (left) and Keith Wallace (right) flank him.

PHOTO BUD FAWCETT.

FIVE LATE '80S BOOM

MEDIA, FAME, MONEY, AND THE NEW PROTECTIONISM

BY THE LATE '80S, SNOWBOARDING HAD REACHED A GROWTH TURNING POINT. INCREASING RESORT ACCEPTANCE, CONTEST SERIES, AND EQUIPMENT IMPROVEMENTS HAD DEVELOPED THE SPORT FROM A PURELY BACKCOUNTRY, MOUNTAIN MAN SCENE TO MORE OF A RESORT-ORIENTED, ACCESSIBLE, COMPETITIVE SPORT WITH ITS OWN MEDIA. GROWTH WITHIN SNOWBOARDING was attracting attention from the outside, in the form of sponsors, speculators, and mainstream media. Money was flowing in from everywhere, but what did that mean for snowboarding? A new tension was brewing, the tension between getting big and staying autonomous. Until the late '80s, this tension surfaced only as a vague fear that the ski industry would take over snowboarding and leave its founders in the dust. But now the danger of outsider interest was becoming more palpable.

Transworld Skateboarding magazine, founded in 1983 by Larry Balma and Peggy Cozens, was the positive alternative to *Thrasher*'s punk rock debauchery and covered snowboarding as a viable winter version of skateboarding. Sims was always bugging *Transworld* to start a snowboarding magazine, and when the World Championships moved from Soda Springs, Lake Tahoe to Breckenridge, Colorado in 1986, the idea finally became feasible. The Breck Worlds brought media from all the country, and between 1986 and 1990, it managed to redefine snowboarding. It was like a revolving door for the heroes of the day, making rock star snowboarders out of Damian Sanders, Shaun Palmer, Bert LaMar, and Craig Kelly.

Damian Sanders remembers: "The Breckenridge Worlds was a huge step. It seems so puny now. The Olympics is a huge step, right? The Worlds was bigger to us. It was everything. The hype started there. They put it on TV." Unlike the Baker Banked Slalom or any of the other contests, Breckenridge was the one where the media came. It was a veritable hype machine for the sport.

According to *Snowboarding Online* editor Lee Crane, snowboarding wasn't really ready for the big time: "They had these big contest sponsors like Swatch, Suzuki, and TDK," he says, "but the organization was terrible. The growth was totally artificial. Everyone thought it was so big, but it was just smoke and mirrors." Pro rider Michele Taggart remembers a similar disparity on a Canadian Pro tour around the same time: "They would drop a lot of money for these purses and no one would come and watch. At the top, we'd all sing, 'three, two one, chaching! drop in, cashing out!' There was so much prize money and so few competitors that we were making money at each gate. Somebody must have lost a bundle." The contest sponsors were the ones losing and often pulled out after one season.

But the Breckenridge World Championships brought enough attention for snowboarding's own media to get started. In 1987, *ISM* was joined on the newsstand by *Transworld Snowboarding,* put out by the publishers of *Transworld Skateboarding.* "The history of any sport begins with the first magazine or the first video," says Kevin Kinnear, founding editor of *Transworld Snowboarding.* "For surfing, it was John Severson making movies in 1960. He started *Surfer* magazine as a program for the movies. Magazines document everything, to the extent that everyone knows who the best are. This leads to heroes."

At the beginning, the snowboarding magazine was made by and for people who were just starting out: "It was very 'This is snowboarding, Come on in!'" says Kinnear of that time. His first story for the magazine was about the Breckenridge Worlds in '87. "I just stood by the half-pipe with a tape recorder and asked everyone about their first day snowboarding, and my old friend Guy Motil, a great surf photographer, took pictures," says Kinnear. "There were probably 35 pros in the world at the time, and most of them were new to the sport as well." *Transworld* kept track of and thereby helped evolve snowboarding's culture. Media makes culture self-conscious, and after the first few issues of the magazine, snowboarding was already evolving into a more mediagenic spectacle.

One of the things that the media communicated from the beginning was that women were competing at a high level. Unlike in surfing or skateboarding, snowboarding seemed to take its cue from skiing, and women muscled into top spots. But any veteran admits that in these early days, winning a women's contest was pretty easy because there was no competition. "It wasn't really about how good you were," says Tina Basich. "It was more that you were a girl and you

Kris Jamieson (center)
with victory checks at
Vision Pro Tour
Championships, 1990.
PHOTO BUD FAWCETT.

Ashild Lofthus, one of the
first consistent winners
among women, at O'Neill
European Championships,
1990. PHOTO ANDREW HOURMONT,
COURTESY JAKE BURTON.

Craig Kelly, winning
the O'Neill European
Championships,
1990. PHOTO PETER MATHIS,
COURTESY JAKE BURTON.

Jeff Brushie and Jason Ford, (who, along with Noah Brandon and Todd Richards, made up the East Coast dream team) at the US Open at Stratton Mountain, Vermont in 1989. PHOTO HUBERT SCHRIEBL, COURTESY JAKE BURTON.

Michele Taggart at the US Open, 1991. PHOTO COURTESY JAKE BURTON.

Nicole Angelrath, winning the Breckenridge Worlds on her first trip to the United States, 1990. PHOTO BUD FAWCETT.

were out there." Young riders like Basich, Michele Taggart, Shannon Dunn, and Nicole Angelrath were getting their starts here at Breckenridge, and would be around to see many changes in women's snowboarding.

"In the '80s, the women were included [in the media] because of their cuteness and their beautiful hair flowing down the mountain," remembers Michele Taggart. With a flash of media interest in the women, it wasn't long before everyone wanted to include a cute girl on their team. In the '80s, still very few women were snowboarding recreationally, but the media attention changed that, which in turn changed snowboarding. While there was a certain amount of tokenism regarding women at that point, women were developing and improving their abilities and would later be appreciated for their skill rather than their femininity.

Madison Avenue and Hollywood started to take an interest in snowboarding as a sparkily novelty. The "extreme" posture was capturing the attention of mainstream media and snowboarding was showing up everywhere, from Wrigley's chewing gum commercials to James Bond movies. These cinematic moments weren't showcasing snowboarding as a real sport though; it was presented more as a stunt. This sort of exposure got a lot of people interested, but in some ways, it was all wrong. The media's representation of snowboarding was a caricature. "The media liked to make it seem like we were all these stupid surfer dudes back then," says Damian Sanders. "I always tried to get the media away from that because it wasn't true. I mean that existed, but not the way the media made it out to be." The outside media distort subcultures to make them more digestible for the uninitiated. Snowboarding would suffer this fate throughout its history. This distortion led to a separation between insiders and outsiders, those who understood the "real" spirit of snowboarding and those who knew only the media version.

Gold Rush Mentality

In the '87-'88 season, Burton and Sims shipped 20,000 and 10,000 snowboards, respectively. These numbers turned heads in the business world and snow-

In 1986, at my first trade show in Europe, we had a booth with Palé, our new manufacturer. This Jamie Salter guy shows up and tells me how he has no real interest in the snowboard industry but he needs to start a new company as a tax write-off. I tried to shoo him away but wasn't successful and Salter offered Palé 2 million to start Kemper. That was when I saw the future. In '88 we just brought it all back home to Seattle and started making boards ourselves again, because I realized that anyone could come in if they had the money, and we had to be more self-sufficient. Salter started this feeding frenzy with Kemper, making everyone think that snowboarding was going to be bigger than it was, and then at the end of the '89 season, everyone had all these boards left and there was a crash. Then the same exact thing happened in '94 with Ride, Salter's newer company, which he put on the Stock Market. He made everyone think that snowboarding was going to take over skiing in a year, and then when everyone threw their money into snowboarding, there was oversaturation *again*. In '95, we saw another crash. Then everyone got a factory. The media keeps trying to pump it, but the hype is all lies, and it hurts the industry.

—Mike Olson, CEO, Mervin Manufacturing

boarding's prospects were suddenly deemed financially viable. Ski and sailboard companies like K2, Rossignol, Look, Kneissl, Atomic, Mistral, and Raichle started to get into the mix, provoking different responses around the industry. "I used to lose sleep over Rossignol," admits Jake Burton. The ski threat was becoming more of a reality. Viewed positively, this outsider involvement served to legitimize and enlarge the consumer base for snowboarding. Viewed skeptically, it was either an evil attempt on the part of skiers to cash in on what they still saw as a fad, or a prophetic warning that snowboarding's independent manufacturing industry would soon be usurped by the larger, more established and conservative industry of skiing. In any case, many industry insiders questioned outsiders' motives. Between the media distortion and industry gold rush, an "us vs. them" seed was planted.

Money was affecting everything. The whole dynamic of professional snowboarding shifted as pros started to earn salaries. Expectations changed, both on the side of the rider and the sponsor. Unmet expectations led to some shifting around. Most notably, when Sims was having trouble with his licenser, Vision Sports, Craig Kelly tried to leave the Sims team for Burton. Sims took Burton to court and Kelly was ordered by a federal judge not to ride any products bearing any logo besides Sims'. Kelly then rode logoless Burton boards until the court reversed the ruling and he signed a long-term contract with Burton. As more and more companies filled the snowboarding industrial landscape, consolidation was placing new demands on pro snowboarders and their sponsors. Riders like Kelly had to switch gears to manage what was now a full-time career, and to think about the future.

In 1989, Junior World Champion Rob Morrow also slid out of his contract with Sims to start his own snowboard company. Launched with family money, Morrow Snowboards was one of the first successful pro-owned companies (along with LaMar). The next year, Vision and Sims went into court, and while Sims was held up in litigation, Morrow hired some Sims people, including Brad Steward, who later launched Bonfire Clothing and ran Salomon Snowboards,

and Scott Clum, who later designed the Raygun Publications snowboarding magazine, *Stick*. Tom Sims felt helpless and betrayed: "I groomed Craig to be my right-hand man, same with Rob and Brad. Opportunity comes for these guys and I couldn't compete. What could I do?" These shifts within the industry marked a generational and developmental turning point in snowboarding.

The main result of the late '80s boom was a new sense of protectionism, both in the industry and on the slopes. Those who had been around since the beginning didn't want to share with strangers, and considered those that were swayed by big money investors to be "selling out." The steady flow of new riders, attracted by the puffed-up "shred dude" media image were scorned by seasoned snow-boarders. "It's like rats in a cage," explains Lee Crane, "when you hit critical mass and they start killing each other. With snowboarding, the vibing started." A rift was created and grew between the insiders and the newcomers. The "real" snow-boarders found that they could not identify with the popular definition of their culture. This eventually led to a major change in snowboarding's identity.

Palmer and I are so different. He's like the dark rebel and I was like the happy, nice-to-everybody kid. We snowboarded together every day, but as we grew up, we were sort of rivals because he was so underground and I was so media-oriented. We went our different ways. Now he comes to my club, Nocturnal Rubber.

—Damian Sanders, pro

You don't want to break the dream. I've made the error in the past, sitting a team rider down and telling him how it is. At the end he has the saddest face. Oz doesn't exist; there's no Santa. The dream is basically what the kids see when they look in the magazines and see Damian or now Terje. They are great lifestyle icons. They have it great. It looks like their lives are 24-hour-a-day adventure. You get handed these plane tickets, you hang out with cool photographers, dye your hair however you want to, and you're making money so your parents have no say in your life. It's all sex, action, and glamour. To an 18-year-old, this is a dream. What the kids don't see is the waiting at the top of the hill in subzero temperatures. Waiting to do the shot, 100 feet, stop, wait, 100 feet, stop, wait, schmoozing at trade shows: it's work.

—Chris Sanders, CEO, Avalanche Snowboards

Hero-worship is a hard thing to deal with, for sure. It's hard to control your ego. You have to make a concerted effort to maintain perspective.

—Craig Kelly, pro

. . . Like me telling people to fuck off and making money and being successful at it. But you gotta be half smart too. You can't pull it if you're a total fucking derelict. It blew up so big. I will always have a big name in snowboarding because of the percentage of people who were doing it when I started. It's just like Tony Hawk, Christian Hosoi, Steve Caballero in skateboarding. They are legends and no one will forget them, like myself, because there were so few people back then. Now there are so many skateboarders and snowboarders, and their names may blow up, but it's not solid, it doesn't have a fucking background or a base like mine.

—Shaun Palmer, pro

I'm a pathetic athlete, which isn't cool. Wrecking hotel rooms doesn't help your snowboarding and it shouldn't help your career.

—Jimi Scott, pro

Yep. I kinda started the whole agent thing. Now a lot of people use my agent. Back in the day you didn't need one. You were making 15K. When I started making more money, I said fuck this, I gotta get an agent. He's an agent for a lot of pro athletes.

—Jeff Brushie, pro

Palmer just got sick of it I think. I mean everyone went to Palmer when they wanted someone to be a dick. And he got to the point, I'm sure, where he just didn't want to do it anymore. Dennis Rodman copied Palmer all the way down. Crossdressing, hair colors, every single thing, Palmer did it five years before Rodman.

—Lee Crane, Editor, *Snowboarding Online*

SIX THREE ICONS

THE NEW ROCK

BY THE TURN OF THE DECADE, SNOW-
BOARDING'S CULTURE AND INDUSTRY
HAD EVOLVED ENOUGH TO PRODUCE ITS
OWN SET OF ICONS OUT OF THE TOP
RIDERS. AS THE MEDIA STARTED TO
PROP THEM UP AND THE KIDS STARTED
TO WORSHIP THEM, PROFESSIONAL RID-
ERS GARNERED MORE POWER. PRO SIG-
NATURE MODEL SNOWBOARDS WERE
MAKING THE SPONSORS SO MUCH
MONEY THAT THEY WERE STARTING TO

listen to the riders about everything. In other words, the riders were starting to drive the whole snowboarding machine, from product development to promotion and media to all-around image. For many, the heightened publicity and adulation turned their hobby into a glamorous and lucrative career, not to mention a full-time job and lifestyle production. Between riding for magazine, video, and catalogue shoots, coaching summer camp, and still getting some contests in, pro schedules were quickly filled up all year long. While the early pros remembered the days of bad equipment and barely enough gas money to get to a contest, all that was changing fast. Pros were starting to travel the world, stay in plush hotels, and sign autographs on a regular basis. Looking at three top snowboarders, Damian Sanders, Shaun Palmer, and Craig Kelly sheds light on different aspects of snowboarding in the transition between the '80s and '90s. All three were heroes to a generation, influencing not just riding style, but the attitudes and values of snowboarding.

Damian Sanders and Shaun Palmer defined the rebellious look and attitude of snowboarding in the late '80s. Growing up in the burgeoning Tahoe freestyle scene, a few years younger than the great Kidwell, Sanders and Palmer came of age just in time for the surge of media coverage in the late '80s. Damian, the younger brother of Avalanche founder Chris Sanders, was perhaps the most visible poster boy of snowboarding's "radical," "extreme" image. He embodied this with everything from clothing to riding style. Spiky hair and Day-Glo head bands were "radical"; every flashy mutation of the board garb was "extreme." In the age of neon, as this period is often called, Day-Glo colors were abrasive, industrial, hardcore. Huge cliff jumps, over-extended postures, gritted teeth, and clenched fists were signs of aggression and in vogue.

Contests were still vital to a pro's standing in the industry, but Sanders and the Avalanche crew were some of the first to actively pursue magazine coverage. What Sanders didn't achieve in competition, he made up for with freeriding shots in magazines. When *Snowboarder* magazine came out in 1989, it was an

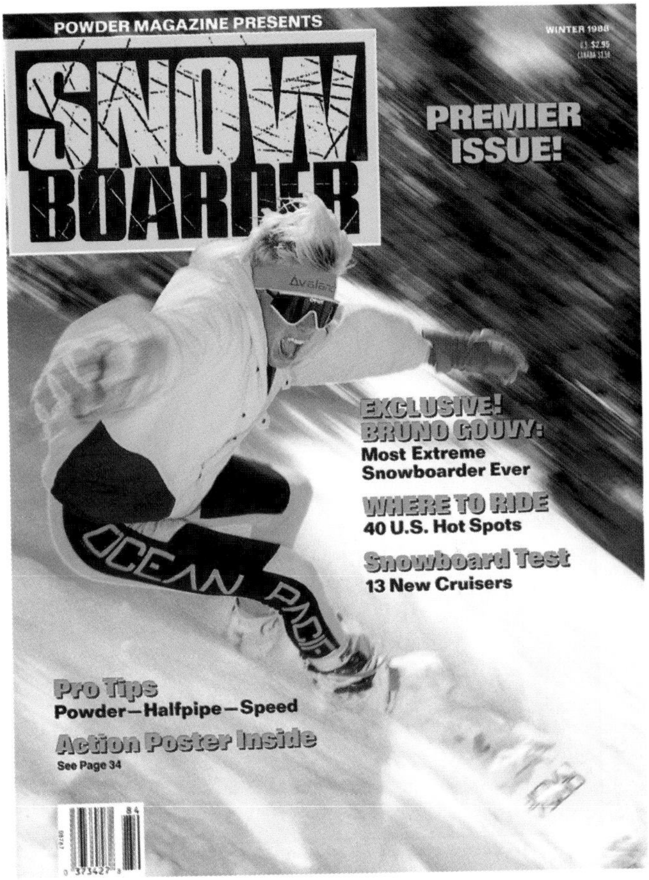
POWDER MAGAZINE PRESENTS
WINTER 1988
SNOW BOARDER
PREMIER ISSUE!
EXCLUSIVE! BRUNO GOUVY:
Most Extreme Snowboarder Ever
WHERE TO RIDE
40 U.S. Hot Spots
Snowboard Test
13 New Cruisers
Pro Tips
Powder—Halfpipe—Speed
Action Poster Inside
See Page 34

The premier issue of *Snowboarder* captures the dominant style of 1988 in Damian Sanders.

aggressive, blurry action shot of Sanders that graced the cover. "I was obsessed with *Thrasher* magazine," says Sanders of that period, "so it was really cool to be in a magazine. I really looked up to skaters like Christian Hosoi. He was a kind of wild, flamboyant pro who was always doing huge airs."

"Aerial acrobatics was Damian's forté," says Sanders' teammate, Tom Burt. "He just wanted to jump. Jumping made him famous, but when videos came in, that put Damian on top of that." Sanders appeared in some of the first big videos, like *Snowboarders in Exile* and *Critical Condition,* with his Lake Tahoe compatriots Steve Graham, Dave Seoane, and Chris Roach. With the snowboard video

Damian with Rob Guistina, 1985. PHOTO BUD FAWCETT.

industry growing, an impressive four-minute segment in a video did as much for a sponsor—and for a career—as winning a major contest.

The videos showcased not only Sanders' talent, but his winning personality and glamorous, carefree lifestyle as well. He was living the dream, and that made him more popular than any contest could have. Image and lifestyle would soon play a bigger and bigger role in professional snowboarding. While Sanders' attitude was authentic, his fashion was totally manufactured: "It was a funny time in my life," says Sanders. "OP started paying me and they were way into the florescent thing. I was totally like Mr. Death Rock in high school and just wanted to wear black and be gnarly looking. It was the total opposite of my style, but they were paying me, and florescent photographed better. The kids who were into snowboarding weren't into death rock, so my black outfits probably wouldn't have worked."

A self-proclaimed "fashion punk," Sanders was unforgettable. He was voted "most extreme snowboarder" in *Transworld*'s reader poll: "The wilder I was the better they liked it," he says. "I was too young to really be conscious of my image, but I would look at magazines and see pictures of European rock stars and want to be like them. My favorite bands were Danzig and Sisters of Mercy." His radical image shaped the way thousands of kids thought about snowboarding.

Sanders' style and attitude would be a little too media friendly for the emerging new school of snowboarding. His ostentatiousness represented everything that would soon be considered passé: mainstream corporate fame (he was even in a McDonald's commercial), big lofty airs, hard boots, and conspicuous, neon clothing. Sanders' legend would live on, beyond the changes in fashion, though. His riding style, a mix of skate-influenced tricks and incorporation of natural terrain would prove to be way ahead of his time. His media sensitivity and image consciousness also foreshadowed the future of snowboarding.

While Sanders' visual style fell out of favor, Shaun Palmer's image thrived. Palmer was snowboarding's first real bad boy. Like John McEnroe in his day, Palmer was cocky, rude, and couldn't lose a contest between 1988 and 1990. While he was at it, he created some of the most lasting images in the history of snowboarding. When people remember those days of competition, they inevitably get a sparkle in their eye, and mention some crazy thing that Palmer did: jumping out a hotel room window, throwing a snowboard into a sacred Japanese bath, flinging a hot dog at a contest organizer, the stories go on and on, and they shaped the image of what it meant to be a real, hardcore, snowboarder.

Sanders at home in the Squaw Valley pipe, 1990. PHOTO BUD FAWCETT.

Unlike most pro snowboarders, Palmer came from a modest background. He started riding at the age of fifteen, when he went to see Chris Sanders at Avalanche. Chris remembers it well: "I was working in my woodshop one night," he says, "and Palmer's little head poked up at the window. Then it disappeared, but I could feel him watching me. So I went out and caught him. He wanted to buy a piece of wood to make a snowboard, I remember, one foot by five foot. He was really determined to snowboard." Palmer was Avalanche's first employee, put to work riveting bindings. He then became a team rider, until he moved on

to the Sims team in 1985, won the junior world championship, and was dubbed "Minishred."

Foul-mouthed and often drinking heavily, Palmer projected a bad attitude that predated that of the new school by many years. "I was a punk," admits Palmer. "I was sneaking into Minor Threat shows when I was 13 and I moved out on my own when I was 16." Palmer was winning enough money to live in a fancy part of South Lake Tahoe. "I was making money from Sims and then cash from contests. I would put the two together, buy drugs, sell them, and double it." Fame and money at such a young age sounds like a recipe for tragedy, but Palmer

Palmer as role model, in the pipe at one of the Mt. Hood snowboard camps, 1991. PHOTO JOHN SPOSETO, COURTESY SIMS.

somehow pulled it off. He would drink and do drugs all night, and win half-pipe contests in the morning.

By the time Palmer won overall at the World Championships at Breckenridge in 1990, he had outgrown the "Minishred" nickname. Instead, he had a huge gothic rendering of "PALMER" tattoed across his abdomen. "The World Championships in '90 was a big high: people screaming my name. It was the peak of contest importance. It changed snowboarding and it changed me. After that, I started drinking, a lot. I just drank and drank." Palmer's drinking didn't stop him from winning though. And his bad attitude was not completely undirected. He was one of the first pros to come out against the lopsided state of snowboarding. Early judges were usually skiers who knew very little about progressive tricks. "I flipped off every judge at some point," he claims. "I was pretty spoiled, I guess. But ask anyone—the judging did suck."

Palmer embodied the rock star ethos: hard drinking and challenging the status quo. "[Jeff] Brushie and I were in Japan for the World Cup and the pipe was so shitty, we couldn't believe it," Palmer recounts. "So we drank all the beers in his little minibar, and something clicked in my mind, like, 'Let's just switch clothes.' No one will know who we are because it was storming out and we had like neck gaiters and shit, so we did that and then we broke into our next door neighbor's room, these Europeans who were staying next door and drank their big ole fuckin' Sapporo beers, too. We got all wasted and went up there in each other's clothes, I don't know, just to be derelicts, I guess." According to people who were there, Palmer got scored better as Brushie than Brushie did as Palmer. Their behavior showed a lack of respect for bad contest organizing. Half-pipe construction became a major issue with snowboarders. Judges rarely knew the difference between a good and a bad half-pipe, and rarely cared. Palmer's attitude was the kick in the pants that snowboarding needed.

Coming from California and growing up in the snowboarding spotlight of Lake Tahoe, Sanders and Palmer were image conscious from the beginning. A few years older and from the Northwest, Craig Kelly was a very different type of icon. Most often categorized as the "soul rider" type, Kelly's mystique has been built around his appreciation for powder and backcountry riding. He isn't an "extreme" rider, although he rides extreme terrain. He isn't a "competitor," although he won the overall world championship (racing and half-pipe) four times in a row. He isn't a movie star, although he has been featured in numerous snowboarding videos, even one or two strictly about him. Craig Kelly was a nerdy engineering student at the University of Washington, who became the best snowboarder in the world and then vanished at just the right time. He is perhaps the most legendary rider in snowboarding.

It is appropriate that this enigmatic rider came from the Northwest. Kelly was part of the original Mount Baker Hard Core, with Jeff Fulton, Carter Turk, and Eric Janko. The difficult weather and varied terrain made great all-around freeriders

of the group. The Northwest had no half-pipes in those days, so Kelly came on the scene with strictly an all-terrain background. He went on a road trip to compete in the '86 Breckenridge World Championships and meet his idol at the time, Terry Kidwell. "Breckenridge was the ultimate journey," says Kelly. "It was a road trip that turned into a career." He ended up moving to Breckenridge soon after because there weren't any contests in the Northwest and Mount Baker was only open three days a week. There was no way to stay home and become a pro snowboarder. "I hated Colorado, but it was a great thing to open my mind and see how it all worked." Kelly figured it out pretty quickly. Winning brought him

Craig Kelly, Blackcomb
Half-Pipe, Canada,
1988. PHOTO BUD FAWCETT.

tons of media attention, but he did not have a notable media persona. "It was a little intense," says Kelly. "I think people got sick of me competing and winning. I got sick of it." There was nothing Kelly couldn't do, but there *were* some things he didn't want to do, and this is what set him apart.

At the peak of his career in 1990, Kelly retired from the competition circuit. "I'm a pretty competitive person, but the way being a pro was going, it was like prostitution." Kelly took snowboarding very seriously and wanted to gain more control over what he did with his sport. He moved from competition to videos. To some, this meant the end of his reign, "Like in Japan, the image of the best snowboarder was the one who wins, so to them I was disappearing," explains Kelly. "But to the kids I came in contact with, and especially to the upcoming pros, it was like the ultimate success. Contest life was hard and not that fun after a while." Kelly retreated back to the Northwest and soon there was a Craig Kelly mystique. While the trend away from competition was bound to happen, due to the growing power of the media and the increasing interest in different types of riding, Kelly's status as a non-competitive pro snowboarder was a living example for other pros to follow.

Instead of competing, Kelly became more influential in his sponsor's design department. "When I started riding for Burton," says Kelly, "they had good racing boards, but their freestyle and freeride boards really sucked. That was a large part of bringing me in. At contests, I would take a hacksaw to the high backs and bolt them on in a weird position and then duct tape my feet to them. Jake was there and it was hard for him to see me do that to his product. But his choice was to either get bummed or let me help him." With very specific ideas about high performance equipment, Kelly had a huge influence on Burton: "Craig taught me a whole lot about listening to team riders," says Burton. "The way I think about my company was influenced a lot by Craig. If I have it my way, the riders will always drive the company and the industry." Kelly could manage his image, ride well, help with R&D, and he was never lazy or late. A true professional, he set a new standard for what can be expected of a rider. From then on, riders who could contribute more to the company than just riding were more valued.

The shift away from organized competition would only become more pronounced in the new school era, but Kelly's personality, public image, and philosophical outlook were what made him a timeless legend. "I dealt with fame in a different way because of where I'm from and because I was already 25 years old," says Kelly. "I had a more rounded view of life than the kids who become famous at 16. I worked. I went to college." His reticence and low-key image iconized a whole new type of pro: the humble ripper. Rather than being cocky, loud, and irresponsible, a lot of Northwest riders—like Jamie Lynn, Dave Lee, and Temple Cummins—who idolized Craig and came up through the pro ranks years later, were shy, polite, and professional.

These riders carried snowboarding from the '80s into the '90s. As some of the earliest and most legendary pros, Sanders, Palmer, and Kelly framed a cultural standard that retains force today. Damian for his image and lifestyle, Palmer for his bad behavior and vocalization, and Kelly for his professionalism and legendary mystique. Of course, none of these image-oriented attributes would have meant a thing if these riders hadn't been incredibly talented and hadn't pushed snowboarding to the next level as a sport. However, all three also influenced snowboarding's ever evolving culture. Worshipped by thousands, they were the first heroes. They put snowboarding on the map and defined the relationships between riders and sponsors, riders and contests, and riders and the public. They rode their way to the center of snowboarding and then drove it right into the American spotlight.

Legendary moment. In the middle of a race at the 1991 OP Pro at June Mountain, Jeff Brushie launches a method: pure rebellion against organized racing.

PHOTO BUD FAWCET.

We called it Big Jean Fantasy. The new school was rebelling, super-rebelling against the ski industry, even rebelling against the established snowboard industry. It was a time against the mainstream. Little did anyone know it would become the mainstream.

—Troy Bush, CEO, Twist/Tuesday/Titan Snowboard Clothing

Southern California was the center of skating and skating was the dominant influence on snowboarding. Who would have ever guessed that skating would be the dominant influence? Skaters and snowboarders did not mix at all. Skaters thought snowboarding was completely gay.

—Kevin Kinnear, Founding Editor, *Transworld Snowboarding*

It was the end of the Burton army. Every time I saw some guy coming down the hill in a Burton suit, mimicking Craig, it made me sick.

—Jason Ford, pro

I was at a ski area association thing and they gave me this gift bag and then I went to take a shit. I looked in the gift bag for some reading material and I pull out this Warren Miller book called *Wine, Women, and Skiing* or something like that. And it talked about all the ski bum antics. Here I was at this ski meeting to address the whole behavior issue in snowboarding and here was Warren Miller's book describing my own generation of skiers behaving the same way when we all were younger. I don't mention it to put that era on a pedestal but it wasn't that different.

—Jake Burton, Founder and President, Burton Snowboards

I remember Dale [Rehberg] and Dave England and Russell Winfield sleeping on the pull-out couch in our office and we would come in to work and they'd be there just waking up and hanging out and smoking pot. It wasn't really like an industry then. We were all just making stuff and people liked it.

—Troy Bush, CEO Twist/Tuesday/Titan Snowboard Clothing

It was the popular kids sport. MTV-ification was in effect. But then too many people could do a 720 off a log.

—Tom Burt, pro

The skateboard guys at *Transworld* were always so microfocused on their trick progression and always put snowboarding down so much for being easier and more accessible. I was always like so they're ollying up a fucking curb, big deal, but now after a couple of years I understand more. Snowboarding is similar.

—Billy Miller, Senior Editor, *Transworld Snowboarding*

I mean in 1990–'91, *everything* was purple and teal. It was awful. Then some trust fund kids got into the mix with more money. You had kids like Dale [Rehberg] and Quinn [Sandoval] wearing anything that showed how different they were from sporto skiers: giant cut-off jeans covered in ice, a huge chain wallet, big hooded sweatshirts, backwards baseball caps, and windbreakers. Then there was the whole gun-toting gangster thing. Every board had a gun on it. Tarquin [Robbins]'s had a shotgun. It came from the whole gangster rap thing, which reached snowboarders before it reached the rest of Colorado. Snowboarders were always more progressive than their surroundings, trendwise.

—Troy Bush, CEO Twist/Tuesday/Titan Snowboard Clothing

They all eventually moved to Southern California to surf and skate. But when we were all in Breckenridge, it was all handrails and hip-hop. Everyone would stay out all night, sliding handrails or partying, and then sleep all day.

—Markus Paulsen, photographer

I had these lame, neon pants that I hated so much. Instead, I would wear three layers of long underwear and regular pants. We were just bored. Like when we cut down the noses of our boards. It was just to see what would happen. It was like being your own board manufacturer instead of having to rely on some company to make something how you want it. There were no boards being made for what we wanted to do anyway, so we took matters into our own hands.

—Jake Blattner, pro

I had artists sending me graphics with snowboarders stabbing skiers with blood everywhere.

—Tom Sims, CEO, Sims Sports

Everyone just snowboarded, all day, every day. There were a lot of drugs and drinking, and trends blew through really quickly. Everyone had dreadlocks, then everyone had a gun, then everyone was a dj. Basically, no one was making any money, even if they were sponsored. But no one really needed money, aside from getting a season pass. Food could be scammed.

—Brad Albert, early Ride rep

It was really just like a big snowboarding high school. . . . There were these things we called "the whales." Every fall they would blow artificial snow into these huge mounds and they were great for making kickers, but the locals, these vibers who hated us at the beginning, thought we were invading them. They called us the East Coast Kicker Kids because we were from east of Colorado. They were the CoBras, which I guess stands for Summit County Brothers, or something like that.

—Dale Rehberg, pro

There weren't really gangs. It was really just something to pass the time. There was the Aryan Regular-footed Army, or if we were on the lift and everyone in front of us was goofy-footed, we'd be like, "Oh TGP, totally goofy posse," but it was really just something else to talk about because all we did was cook pizzas and snowboard.

—Jake Blattner, pro

One day I went up to Brad Steward and asked him what was up with the powder sucks t-shirts. He said the kids hate powder because they can't go jibbing. They can't even ride powder. I thought, "I can't believe it's come to this." I'm glad that's over, to be honest with you.

—Tom Sims, CEO, Sims Sports

Aaaarh, [core] is a really obscure thing to try and define. When I use the term hardcore, I'm talking about a kid who's going to go buy something that's designed and owned by people who sponsor the most influential riders of the time. Typically, it's a small company like us, not a big company like Quiksilver.

—Ken Block, owner, Circus Distribution and original publisher/editor of *Blunt*

SEVEN BACKLASH AND BOOM AGAIN

THE NEW SCHOOL

ALL THE MONEY, MEDIA, AND NEON OF THE LATE '80S AND THE RESULTING RIFT BETWEEN INSIDERS AND NEWCOMERS SPIRALED INTO A NEW IDENTITY FOR SNOWBOARDING. ALTHOUGH KIDWELL'S LEGACY HAD BEEN DOING SKATE TRICKS SINCE THE EARLY '80S, THERE WAS AN EMERGING UNDERGROUND "NEW SCHOOL," WHO WERE QUICK TO ADAPT THE CURRENT AGGRESSIVE STREET

style of skating to snowboarding. Earth tones, oversized street clothes, and beanie hats replaced neon, ski clothes, and headbands. Flatland spinning tricks and rail slides replaced lofty aerials. Behavior became increasingly outrageous. In the most intense period of skier-snowboarder conflict, the media churned out sensationalized reports of gang wars on the hill—snowboarders carrying guns, dealing drugs, and threatening innocent skiers. The tension between snowboarders and skiers was by no means new, but with more and more snowboarders, both sides became less tolerant. Snowboarders were getting the reputation that skateboarders had been enjoying for years: they were officially declared a menace. Much as skateboarding and surfing ended their association in the late '70s, snowboarding separated from skiing and took on the increasingly urban, aggressive attitude of skateboarding in the early '90s.

Street Skating Roots Movement

Skateboarding has been through a few cycles of underground movement followed by mainstream prosperity. In the early '60s, the first skateboarders in Southern California were frustrated surfers; when the ocean was flat, they killed time "sidewalk surfing" on two-by-fours with metal wheels. The next peak in the '70s focused on slalom and pool skating, which though at first was daring and renegade, became formalized and conventional as parks were built and skating became big business. The early '80s brought a slump, followed by the popularization of vert half-pipe skating, accompanied by a small roots movement on the street, which grew and lasted throughout the '80s. This is the period when snowboarders looked up to and emulated vert skaters, like Steve Caballero and Christian Hosoi.

The new street skating of the '80s was no "sidewalk surfing"; it was an aggressive synthesis of tricks and speed that used all the existing obstacles in the street environment. In the early '90s, the "new school" in skateboarding used smaller boards and smaller wheels to allow more technical flatland tricks. Based on the "handless aerial" or "ollie" (invented by vertical skater Alan Gelfand) and the urban landscape, new school skaters used sidewalks, stairs, handrails, and fountains. The urban environment also catalyzed to the age-old connection between skaters and trouble. Skaters were now a public hazard, destroying public property, listening to loud hip-hop music, writing graffiti, endangering old ladies on the sidewalks, and mouthing off at cops. The attitude of the skate underground was one of exclusivity and their traditional stance as outsiders only intensified. They took pride in being indecipherable to the mainstream.

The Ghetto

The locus of the new school's development was in the ski resorts of Summit County, Colorado: Copper Mountain, Breckenridge, and Arapahoe Basin. Ever since the World Championships moved to Breckenridge in 1986, the area had been in the spotlight. Filmmakers and still photographers went there to shoot, and pros and wannabe pros went there to live out the snowboarding dream. Summit County was the place to become a pro in the early '90s. Snowboarders migrated in posses to Breckenridge from all over the country, looking for a way to get sponsored.

One such group of kids came from the flatlands of Wisconsin in 1991, and truly changed the face of snowboarding. Dale Rehberg, Nate Cole, Jake Blattner, and Roan Rogers are names synonymous with the new school. They grew up skiing and snowboarding in the Midwest, where the mountains are small and cold. "Coming from Wisconsin, we didn't know anything about big mountain riding," says Jake Blattner. "We used to build jumps, tow each other behind the car,

anything that seemed fun." The limitations of small mountains led these kids to experiment. While moving to Breckenridge gave them more powder than they had ever seen, they continued to experiment. Jibbing—or jumping off an obstacle to do a skate trick—was the main attraction, and in Breckenridge the obstacles ranged from stumps and rocks to snowblowers, signage, parked cars, and picnic tables.

Experimentation didn't stop with riding style. They also experimented with equipment, chopping off the tip and tail of their boards (supposedly to reduce swing weight), and taking the high backs off of their bindings to make their snowboards more like skateboards. The new school was about tricks, not powder. The philosophy of the era was distinctly DIY (do-it-yourself). Says Jake Blattner: "There was nothing being made for what we wanted to do, so instead of waiting around for snowboarding to catch up, we just took matters into our own hands."

> Dale Rehberg at Arapahoe Basin. Joyride was the first favorite of the new school set, shown here with T-bolts, used to widen stance. PHOTO JUSTIN HOSTYNEK

**Tarquin Robbins,
Arapahoe Basin, 1992.**
PHOTO JUSTIN HOSTYNEK.

**Jay Nelson, nighttime
rail sliding, 1992.** PHOTO
JUSTIN HOSTYNEK.

**Kurt Wastell, Bear
Mountain, 1993.** PHOTO
MARKUS PAULSEN.

**Bryan Iguchi,
Tyrol Basin,
Wisconsin 1994.**
PHOTO JEFF CURTES.

Back in the '70s, most skaters identified with one of a few major companies, and contests were popular. With the new street trend, they became more tribe-like, rallying around the smaller, pro-rider-affiliated companies, and contests were scorned. Magazines like *Thrasher,* and then *Transworld Skateboarding* and *Big Brother* showcased the new smaller companies and created a revolving door of new media heroes. Skate companies also made videos to showcase their riders. With virtually no structure of competition to bring participants together to influence each other, skateboarding relied more and more on the media to define and promote the ever-changing image landscape of the sport.

Snowboarding in the early '90s mirrored skateboarding. An outsider stance, anticorporate values, avoidance of contests, and a search for alternate ways to ride full time, all drove the new school in snowboarding. Tom Sims sees the early '90s as a replica of the early '80s: "In the early '80s, skateboarding became urban and punk. Then it seeped out to the suburbs. A decade later, there was a resurgence of punk in skating and snowboarding. This is when snowboarding finally became cool in skaters' eyes."

This is really when snowboarding broke through the cool barrier. No more neon. No more dorky ski stuff. With the more hardcore, urban style of street skaters, new school snowboarders could not be mistaken for skiers. As the skate attitude and fashion spread, snowboarding became popular. In the first half of the 1990s, snowboarding hit the mainstream, capturing the youth of America.

SoCal Nation

Kids everywhere were running out to buy snowboards, but nowhere was snowboarding exploding more than in Southern California. Since the surf fantasy era in the '60s, the stretch of land between Malibu and La Jolla had been a trend mill for youth culture, exporting surf and then skate culture to the world. The established infrastructure of manufacturers and magazines positioned SoCal as the obvious home for the snowboarding industry and its official culture. The SoCal

Ride

In 1992, venture capitalist Jamie Salter (remember him from Kemper?) and former Burton team manager Tim Pogue put their heads together to create Ride Snowboards. With Salter's financial savvy and Pogue's cultural savvy, there was no stopping Ride; they made new school equipment (short, twin-tip boards with inserts for extra wide stances) and hired almost the entire Breck crew to ride for them: Dale Rehberg, Roan Rogers, Russell Winfield, superstar Jason Ford, and comer Circe Wallace. At their first trade show, Pogue put up a skateboard quarter-pipe, the essence of coreness in 1992. The word out at the time was that Pogue left Burton, "the corporate giant of snowboarding" to start this underdog company that would be true to the riders.

Behind the curtains, Jamie Salter was making the deals. He worked his connections so that at the very first trade show, Ride was offering bags, gloves, boards, hats, summer camp, everything. And for cheap. None of the product was very high quality, but the boards were good shapes and it was *what people wanted*. Ride sold well at its first trade show and Salter strategically went public with the company. He wooed Wall Street by showing the suits snowboarding's rapid growth figures and Ride shot up to the #2 growth position on the market. Shares went from $2 to $35 in 18 months; and sales reached 75 million dollars.

Within a few years, the stock was down, and both Pogue and Salter walked away from Ride . . . millionaires. Pogue was quoted in the *Wall Street Journal* as saying, "The numbers that everybody wanted and the reality of what Ride could do were two different things. It wasn't about snowboarding anymore. It was about pleasing Wall Street." While Ride made price point boards for a huge new market and gave the industry a challenging taste of the future, its values went against everything that snowboarding stands for: creating hype, taking short-term profits, and selling out.

matrix of the tri-sport scene—surfing, skating, snowboarding—was so well-attuned to everything surrounding the actual act of snowboarding that the home base of snowboarding didn't even need to be near the snow. During this boom period, snowboarding forged its own cohesive industry, fashion, and media; and it gained full control of its own image for the first time. What better place for this powerful image to set up court than in the center of skate culture, Southern California?

Sport specific clothing that distinguished snowboarders from skiers was first on the new school agenda. Just as the kids were flocking to Breckenridge in '91 (see the Ghetto section), a snowboarder/graphic designer named Ken Block was moving from Breckenridge to SoCal to start a skate clothing company called Droors. In the style of skateboarding's new school, Block's clothes were over-sized and heavily influenced by hip-hop. "The Kicker kids used to wear the jeans I made for snowboarding," he reports, "so in like '92 or '93, I bought some waterproof nylon from Raul Reise and made some waterproof jeans." It was the dawn of a whole new era for snowboarding clothes.

"Gotcha and Billabong and Quiksilver had been making snowboard clothing for a long time, but, that stuff was like florescent ski gear for snowboarders," continues Block. "I hate to use the term hardcore, but with the hardcore influence of snowboarding that was coming out of Breckenridge at the time, kids wanted to look like skaters, not skiers. A lot of companies developed out of that." It wasn't until the new "hardcore" companies came out that snowboarding hit the big time, appealing to skaters and skater wannabes who could relate to the skate style and put it all together.

Block says that the revolt against the ski industry affected where snowboards were sold. "Until like '91, snowboards were only sold in ski shops. Burton, Mistral, Kemper, those were the brands. Then suddenly, there ware these skate-influenced companies, like Type A, Special Blend, Joyride, and even Ride. These companies got the attention of skate shop owners and the next thing you

Norwegian-born Terje Haakonsen, pictured here on his first pro model in 1994, is a snowboarder in a class by himself. At the 1995 Baker Banked Slalom, he dropped into the course fakie and still won. After that, there was no stopping him. Often jumping eight to nine feet out of the half-pipe, Haakonsen was dubbed the "Michael Jordan of Snowboarding."

PHOTO TREVOR GRAVES.

Stevie Alters, after slamming his face into a log in Vail, 1994. PHOTO MARKUS PAULSEN.

kn[e]w, snowboards and snowboard clothing [were] being sold in skate shops."
At the skate shops, Burton and Kemper were scorned, and the smaller, hardcore companies just took over. None of the kids wanted the big, ski shop brands, they wanted the most obscure, skate-inspired product on the market.

Also in '91, an ex-pro surfer named Richard Woolcott quit his promotions job at Quiksilver. He had just been to Lake Tahoe during an epic spring dump and all he wanted to do was snowboard. Woolcott and his friend Tucker Hall started Volcom as an experiment; they silkscreened a few t-shirts and took off on a huge snowboarding tour. Wolcott was living off royalties for surfing in a TV commercial for Budweiser, and that pretty much sustained him until the spring of '93, when he and Hall were finally making a whole line of casual clothing. "I remember driving down the freeway with our first set of shorts and there were tanks coming the other way because the LA riots were going on," recalls Woolcott. "Kurt Cobain had just killed himself and I felt like there was a lot going wrong." In the punk tradition, the slogan for Volcom is "Youth Against Establishment." Their early graphics were in the same vein as the late Sex Pistols' graphics.

Volcom developed more like a family than a clothing company. Woolcott and Hall's brotherly attitude and antimainstream cry struck a chord with a very intense scene of kids in Southern California. "It's tribes like Volcom that have replaced the nuclear family," says Lee Crane. "They offer membership." From skateboard, to snowboard to surf teams, Volcom still regards its athletes as family. "We try to create an environment in which people can forget about all that's wrong with the world and have fun," says Woolcott, unintentionally echoing the surfers of the Vietnam era.

The fact that Volcom doesn't make any outerwear, and yet is recognized as a major cultural producer is a testament to the current strength of the tri-sport lifestyle. "Clothing is a minor part of it," says Woolcott. "The art side of what we do is the most important. When the kids get it, it's meaningful." Woolcott's philosophy seeps into everything Volcom does, from their videos (some of the most highly regarded snowboarding videos in the industry) to their book of black and white snowboarding photography. His authentic commitment to the surf/skate/snow lifestyle garners him credibility in all three industries.

The new school era resulted in a new boom for snowboarding that echoed the boom in the late '80s, only this time it was much louder. With its own industrial and media infrastructure, developed in the vein of new school skateboarding, snowboarding's numbers skyrocketed and culturally it came down from the mountains and into urban areas. The ghost of skiing was finally killed by the per-

Snowboarding brought on a revival in vert skateboarding. John Cardiel, padless McTwist at the first Diesel Contest Riksgransen, Sweden, 1994.

PHOTO MARKUS PAULSEN.

vasive new urban skate style. Even though snowboarding seemed to take a lot from skating during this period, it was only part of a larger cycle of evolution that would soon move back to the mountains. In the meantime, the boom allowed for a lot of creative experimentation and with so much interest from a varied array of outside sources, the culture was simultaneously more unique and more cosmopolitan than ever before.

Kris Jamieson, pro:

I've been snowboarding for so long, it begins to blur. I look at my friends sometimes and I think, "How come some people are making so much money and some so little?" It just goes to show you that snowboarding is just like any other capitalist venture. People don't get what they deserve. They get what they negotiate.

Snowboarding isn't different than say, being a stockbroker?

No. Snowboarding, essentially, is a cool race. Everyone stands around trying to be cool. And coolness is a skill. Cool people aren't lucky. It's a skill. It's the skill of being able to limit your actions. You limit your freedom to yell things at people. If you went off all the times you wanted to, people would not think you were cool.

That's how you succeed in snowboarding?

Well these cool snowboarders were by no means the best snowboarders, and if you threw them into a contest they'd get their asses kicked. Snowboarding became a completely image-based sport. But nowadays, it's changing again. Contests are more important again. If you can't prove yourself in competition, the future may be shaky for you.

How would you decide who was best?

I think there should be a personality test. People need to want to be a pro snowboarder with all of its parts. Not just the "cool" stuff. It's customer service. Sometimes I feel like riders don't deserve to have the jobs they have.

Max Jenke and Devun Walsh over TJ Liese's tracks. Tyax, Whistler, Canada. PHOTO JUSTIN HOSTYNEK.

EIGHT THE MEDIA TAKES OVER

IMAGE RULES

DURING THE NEW SCHOOL ERA, MAGA-
ZINES AND VIDEO PICKED UP WHERE
CONTESTS LEFT OFF AS THE GREAT PER-
COLATORS FOR ALL THINGS SNOW-
BOARDING. WHILE *TRANSWORLD
SNOWBOARDING* WAS AT THE TOP,
SNOWBOARDER (PUT OUT BY SURFER
PUBLICATIONS) WAS DEVELOPING A
STRONG FOLLOWING AS THE MORE
ANTI-ESTABLISHMENT OF THE TWO. DUE

to the overwhelming number of new snowboard-related companies, the two SoCal-based magazines exploded with advertising pages. "It was like McDonald's in our ad department," says *Snowboarder*'s publisher, Doug Palladini. "We got to the point where we were just taking orders—no selling at all." Both *Transworld* and *Snowboarder* grew to the size of small phone books.

It was the right place and the right time. The media were now driving the sport. Lee Crane, one of the early editors of *Transworld Snowboarding* explains: "Manufacturers realized, 'We don't have to have the best guy. We just have to have the coolest, and we can make a hero out of him in the magazines and in videos.' It's kind of a scam. With surfing, Kelly Slater is the best and he proves it every week, but with snowboarding, it's just who's the coolest right now. It's a lot cheaper to just pick a cute, cool, one-of-many instead of fighting for one of the top three."

"The magazines got so powerful because of the nature of our audience," says Palladini. "Snowboarders are passionate consumers. For them, the magazines are not just something you pick up at the airport. To the core, it is the bible. Companies were spending up to 50% of their budgets on advertising. In most industries, they spend 5%. Snowboarding is a completely image-based sport and the most direct line to kids is through our magazines."

"Ads are where you get respect," says Ken Block, who built his skate/snowboard clothing empire during this period. "If a company knows what's going on, it'll be reflected in the ad and kids can see that. If they are trying to act like they know what's going on but they don't, kids see through them and won't buy the product." Marketers' main goal at this point was to achieve public perception as authentic. Ads were their big chance to show their insider status.

Disillusioned with the standards of the existing two magazines, Ken Block launched *Blunt* for the hardcore snowboarder in 1993. "My friends who were skaters would look at the supposed bible, *Transworld,* and laugh because they

Pro rider Wes Makepeace. This shot was used as a *Blunt* **contents page. PHOTO MARKUS PAULSEN.**

were mislabeling tricks. They were teaching misinformation. We were really into *Big Brother,* a new skate mag at the time that was really raw, totally uncensored." Block's goals for *Blunt* were the same: to be a totally raw, totally uncensored voice in the industry that spoke to the most progressive hardcore snowboarders. "We appealed to the male between the ages of 16 and 21, who liked to drink, look a certain way, and ride a certain way," he says. *Blunt* appealed to the derelict snowboarders, and anyone who was sick of the fresh-faced, squeaky clean look of the dominant magazines.

Blunt's use of video grabs instead of sequence shots was indicative of the period. The video industry had exploded with the successes of Mac Dawg's (aka Michael McIntire) "The Hard, the Hungry and the Homeless" and "New Kids on the Twock." Video was the proclaimed future of snowboarding, showing the sport in it's purest form—action. "It was a trendy thing to do," Block admits. "*Transworld Skateboarding* was doing it, *Big Brother* was doing it. It was all about the truth. Just like we corrected the mislabeling of tricks, we used video because video doesn't lie. *Transworld Snowboarding* was showing these sequences where the guy wasn't even landing the trick. *Blunt* always showed the guy riding away." Total authenticity was more important to the hardcore skateboarder-snowboarder than most magazine editors at the time realized. Correctly naming tricks and showing their completion was the goal . Advertising only the hardcore companies and selling only in skate shops, *Blunt* represented the power of the new school aesthetic. Block turned *Blunt* over to the publishers of *Big Brother* after a year or two, and then in 1997, Larry Flynt bought both *Big Brother* and *Blunt.*

Block wasn't the only one taking matters into his own hands, media-wise in the mid-'90s. Magazines spawned as fast as companies at this point: *Plow, Stick, Heckler, Fresh and Tasty, Medium, Eastern Edge, East Infection, Strength, Snowboard Life,* and a host of other smaller magazines surfaced all over the country to cover their own scenes in a way they thought was authentic, and if possible, to reap as many of the new ad dollars as they could.

Image-Makers

Photographers and filmmakers grew in number accordingly, injecting new perspectives and images into the system, as well as new riders. "The one thing that can really propel a scene or a rider into the spotlight is a photographer," says Kevin Kinnear, founding editor of *Transworld Snowboarding.* "A good photographer can be very powerful." Photographers are the real image-makers. Their work creates the dream that is snowboarding. It sells the lifestyle.

The top photographers live the fantasy as much as the riders. They jet around all season, not to trade shows or demos, but to the most exciting spots: the best contests, the most private powder stashes, and the most exotic peaks. Their friendships with riders are more than the usual athlete-photographer relationship. On the road, riders and photographers essentially live together. For both, snowboarding is much more than a job. It's a life. Top snowboarding photographer Trevor Graves explains: "If you're shooting to maintain the lifestyle, it's worth it," he says. "That's all you can do with the time constraints anyway. It's not a huge cash-maker, like fashion or rock photography. It's really about living snowboarding."

With the rise of the video industry, snowboarding's hero-worship system intensified. "The film thing is more powerful right now," agrees Graves. "Before, print was the only way. Now if you're on the film list, you're in with the kids and the industry, then the mags and the broader spectrum kicks in. Print supports the video." Manufacturers make their own videos and also sponsor independent filmmakers. Snowboarders, like skaters, watch videos over and over, either to learn tricks, or just to check out the newest, most progressive riders in action.

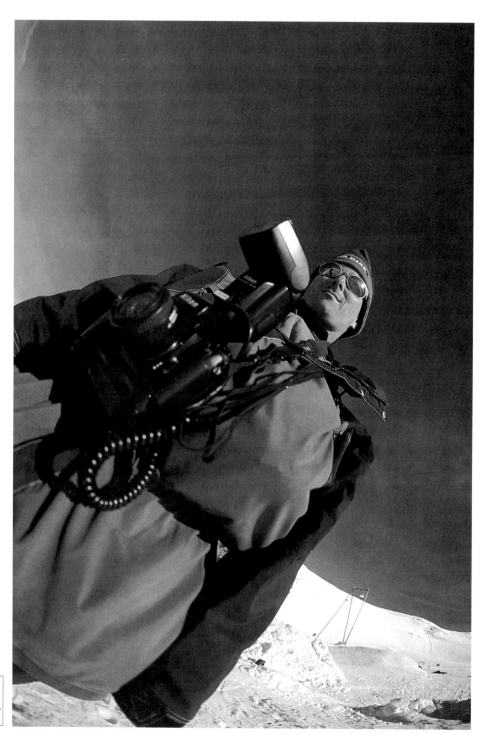

Photographer Trevor Graves on the job in Zermatt, Switzerland.
PHOTO JEFF CURTES.

The politics of judging competitions was replaced by the politics of acquiring and controlling media coverage. Who was photographed, wearing what clothes, on whose board became of utmost importance to the advertiser-dependent media; and the swag (or free stuff) system went haywire. Armies of public relations and marketing people were hired to get the stuff in the right hands, as snowboarding's financial expectations reached a fevered pitch. Maintaining growth in the face of market saturation was becoming a difficult challenge for both the industry, and therefore the media.

Mt. Hood, Oregon is the center of American snowboarding in the summer. Often referred to as "Hollyhood," it draws cameras from all over. Daniel Franck, being heavily mediated.
PHOTO AARON SEDWAY.

(s i c k)

Inside media: Filmmaker and star of early videos, Dave Seoane and rider Bryan Iguchi, on the set of *Roadkill.* PHOTO BUD FAWCETT.

kennedy @ brd aid III

CB96

Outside media: MTV's
Kennedy with pro rider
Dave Lee at Board Aid III,
a snowboarding festival
to raise money for AIDS
research. **Big Bear,
California.** PHOTO JARED
EBERHARDT.

Between the four of us, the word "alternative" was kept in heavy rotation, and lame Gen X puns were dropped like business cards. We were going to a festival concert to be with our people, and yet had more spite than the frugal gourmet. The concert was designed as a buffet platter of new toys, forbidden fruits, exotic delights. You were supposed to feel like an insider, somebody with an edge on life. In its fourth year, I think my friend Dan summed it up by pointing out, "Lollapalooza is just a really big t-shirt stand with good music and stage lighting."

—from Lollapalooza concert report by Mark Lewman in *Big Brother* issue #13

NINE ALTERNATIVE CULTURE AND SNOWBOARDING

THE YEAR THAT PUNK BROKE

THE NEW SCHOOL BOOM REFLECTS SNOWBOARDING'S PARTICIPATION IN AND MERGING WITH A LARGER PROCESS IN AMERICA: THE MAINSTREAMING OF THE "ALTERNATIVE." ALONGSIDE AND ENTWINED WITH SNOWBOARDING, UNDERGROUND YOUTH CULTURE SUR-FACED AND EVOLVED RAPIDLY IN THE EARLY '90S. WHILE THE MOST OBVIOUS indicators of alternative youth culture are the outward fashions of rave, roots, skate, grunge, hip-hop, punk, *and* snowboarding, each of these styles carry with it a range of identity-forming values and attitudes. These attitudes joined together in the '90s under the umbrella term "alternative."

In the process of mainstreaming, the term has changed drastically. When I was in junior high in the mid '80s, "alternative" referred to a certain type of college rock, exemplified by R.E.M. and the Talking Heads. Alternative music was trying to separate from rock's formulaic industry. Usually a little arty, usually a little smart, the scene thrived on not being popular, obvious or particularly consumable. This is the backbone to an otherwise constantly changing culture. Before long, the meaning of "alternative" broadened. There were more bands with increasingly diverse (often contradictory) musical styles, fashions and philosophies (Red Hot Chili Peppers, Phish, Beck, Mudhoney), all being promoted as "alternative." At best, this hybrid nature was subversively tolerant of mixing different ideas. At worst, it was just fuzzy thinking, ripe for marketing exploitation. By the mid '90s, the idea of alternative was a craze, coveted most by large soft-drink companies, television stations, major record labels—all things mainstream—that wanted to don the authenticity and independence associated with the increasingly popular "alt" stance.

Snowboarding contributed to the growth and eventual mainstreaming of alternative culture. It too moved from a specific taste group to the wider market, where snowboarding had become a symbol of hipness. Its roots in outsider sports (surfing and skateboarding), 'rebel' status at ski resorts, and edgy associations with the (increasingly popular yet often banned) hardcore hip-hop and gangster style secured snowboarding's identity as alternative.

While there are many vehicles for alternative values, the Beastie Boys and Nirvana have made them accessible on an iconic scale. The Beastie Boys' DIY, entrepreneurial spirit (they run a record label, a magazine, and influenced the birth of a clothing line), hybrid tastes (hardcore, hip-hop, and lounge music), and mixture of authenticity and irony (they make fun of all that they love, from their urban roots to '70s cop shows) are major components of alternative culture. Nirvana's authenticity is similar, but more adamantly non-urban. The late Kurt Cobain's songs were alternately poppy and abrasive, self-parodying, yet encased in an authentic cry. Cobain's music was laden with misery, but his public persona betrayed an unwillingness to take himself seriously: a contradiction, but a common one. Cobain hated mainstream rock, yet his band's records went platinum. His sarcasm acknowledged the contradictions, and thereby dissolved them. Nirvana and the Beastie Boys, two markedly different bands, exemplified many of the same values, and their successes were a testament to the strength and popularity of alternative culture in the '90s.

Similarly, snowboarders sampled from different cultures and styles, both urban and nonurban, crude and subtle, idealistic and opportunistic, straddling the contradictions being sincere and being ironic about the messages and values they were mixing. This melding of opposites and unpredictable shifting of personal image, so much a part of snowboarding, was also at the crux of alternative identity.

Alterna-fests like Lollapallooza brought together both disparate musical genres and formerly conflicting cultures of ravers, skaters and computer nerds—all together under one tent. It was a hotbed of multi-culti, hybrid fashions. While some kids were very careful and meticulous about their ensembles, others sampled without intention: techno fashion with skate company logos, along with piercings (neo-tribal), tattoos, gold teeth (hip-hop), and a beanie hat (snowboarding) *all on the same person*. The intricate language of cultural sampling and membership was largely encoded in logos. Status in the alternative is based on *understanding* the nuances of the culture. To the initiated member, decoding a combination of t-shirt graphics and other visual signifiers such as tattoos, piercings and hair configuration was an automatic and unconscious evaluation.

In spite of all the mixing to stay unique, the marketing wheels of larger companies raced to capture the image-conscious Lollapalloozer market. Trendspotters infiltrated skate parks, school yards, and concerts to find out what the cool kids would want next. A homogenized "alternative" style resulted. Enter Urban Outfitters: buy five items and be cool. Alternative culture was being reduced to mere fashion.

Retaining integrity in the face of fashion became difficult. Snowboarding also underwent continual shifts of nuance to stay ahead of being known, understood and co-opted. In 1995, the snowboarding booths at the Ski Industries trade show were mostly chainlink fences and graffitied walls, with old vintage sofas and skate ramps. These urban and grunge images communicated the small, anti-corporate identity of an insider or "core" company, while slickness was associated with skiing or corporate snowboarding. But after a while, the distressed, street pose was recognized by insiders as just that, empty posturing. Snowboarding was becoming a caricature of itself. In an effort to regain authenticity, trendsetters moved away from the traditional rebellions of piercing and tattooing and toward a more conservative and *ironically* mainstream stance, with less visual signification, more technically functional clothing, and an overall decrease in identification with the stereotyped "snowboarder." The chainlink fences disappeared around '97. Just as words like "shred" and "dude" had been co-opted to the point of ridicule, terms like "jib," "core," and "alternative" were becoming a joke, only to be used with "extreme" irony.

Jamie Lynn, tagging the top of a big air jump in London, England, 1996. PHOTO CHRIS BRUNKHART.

They said "no girls allowed," and we were like, "Oh we're for sure doing it now." But then we looked at it; it was really sketchy, like a 60-foot jump. We went and put on all pink and pigtails and we were listening to the Beastie Boys and trying to get all amped up. There were like 100 stairs to the top of the jump. We walked halfway up and stopped. Then I don't remember walking the rest of the way up, but I did not hesitate. I took three breaths and then dropped.

—Tina Basich, pro, describing a Big Air contest that she and Shannon Dunn bum rushed in 1994.

At Airwalk I was the only female in upper management. It was all board meetings with 40 men in suits and me. Then there was this surge of interest in women and all of these women were walking in and saying "I'm a woman and I deserve all of this," and I had a hard time with that, because I had earned my position through hard work and compromise.

—Lisa Hudson, Promotions Director, Twist Snowboard Clothing

They like to party late. We take shooting really seriously in snowboarding, but the fashion photogs are used to models who stay up all night and sleep all morning. When we did this shoot for *Bazaar,* I was pounding on Mario [Sorrenti]'s door yelling in the morning. It wasn't raining yet, but he couldn't get up until noon and it was raining by then. Fashion magazines generally misrepresent snowboarding anyway. And even the snowboarding media try to make role models out of women, but women don't have female role models—that's why they have more of their own identity. Women don't want to be just like other women. They are competitive. Why do boys worship men so much? Men in snowboarding look the same, have the same mannerisms, talk the same, ride the same. I can't distinguish between them—and I'm inside the sport.

—Morgan Lafonte, pro

TEN THE WOMEN

CHICKS DIG IT

THERE IS NO FEMALE EQUIVALENT TO
SHAUN PALMER BECAUSE WOMEN
AREN'T LIKE MEN IN SNOWBOARDING.
HISTORICALLY, THEY HAVEN'T HAD THE
POWER TO MISBEHAVE; THEY WERE
CONSIDERED (A) BRAVE TO BE OUT
THERE RIDING WITH THE GUYS, AND (B)
LUCKY TO BE INCLUDED. IT WASN'T
UNTIL THE EARLY MID-'90S EXPLOSION
IN THE WOMEN'S RECREATIONAL MARKET
THAT FEMALE PROS STARTED MAKING A

lot of money for their sponsors and moved into the limelight as the darlings of the industry. Garnering more respect and slowly closing the male-female ability gap, women are becoming lifestyle icons to the younger generation, representing strength, grace, skill, and ambition. As the first wave of women get more and more comfortable and confident in an industry of men, a new generation of female rippers is in the pipe, practicing. And as we approach this new generation's coming of age, it's interesting to take a look back at how the perception of women in snowboarding has evolved.

Back in the day, in an industry with no women pro models and no sport-specific (never mind women-specific) clothing to speak of, girls were tokens on each team. Early pros like Jean Higgins, Suzi Riggins, and Tara Eberhard-Masterpool were good athletes and stretched the limits placed on women, but the younger set of pioneers, like Tina Basich, Shannon Dunn, and Michele Taggart bridged the gap between women as tokens and women as viable pro athletes.

In 1986, Tina Basich hiked up the back of Soda Springs in Lake Tahoe wearing moon boots. It was her first day snowboarding. The image of her laughing while trying to keep her feet in the boots is emblematic of the early years. Another image from that time is of Michele Taggart, crashing but still winning her first half-pipe contest. At that point, there was nothing to lose and very little to gain by getting into the sport. Both women started competing in the late '80s for the sheer fun of it with no clue that they would one day make six-figure salaries and be famous around the world. Basich says that snowboarding was the first and only thing that made her comfortable about who she was. Over the course of her career, she would pass on the favor. Basich and others like her helped girls feel good about making sports the center of their lives. She helped carve them a space in the culture, a place where they could develop their own strong, independent identities in a nontraditional way.

A diverse matrix of trends came together at the right time to create a major turning point in women's snowboarding. For many years, girls who snowboarded were like girls who skated—not taken very seriously in the media or marketplace. Tina Basich and Shannon Dunn were two tomboys who won contests. When Kemper and Sims came out with their pro women's models in '94, no one thought they would sell. But the timing was perfect. The girls who had always been interested in skating (but were never encouraged), found a more inclusive scene in snowboarding. Gender-specific boards helped legitimize their new-found place.

It was a time for celebration. Girls rushed out to buy a board made especially for them: shorter, lighter, and narrower, with more flex. Coincidentally, boys wanted a board like this for doing the new school tricks, so the Basich and Dunn pro models sold overwhelmingly well. This produced a waterfall of interest in girls, both recreationally and professionally. They were suddenly being touted by forecasters as the fastest growing market in snowboarding. For better deals, Basich moved to Sims and Dunn to Burton, where they became the highest paid women in snowboarding.

Sensing the groundswell, the two women launched a women's clothing line with their clothing sponsor, Swag in 1994. It was called Prom. "No one believed that any of it would work," says Basich. "We wanted to start a girls' line because at the time, all the boys' clothes were super-huge, the new school style. We couldn't find clothes to wear. Then when we were designing it, we realized that the line was going to look like a boys' extra small so we decided to go totally over-board. We called it Prom and wore prom dresses in the ads and made it all pastel colors. We had to make fun of the whole girl thing to get noticed as something different." Indeed, the Prom image made a splash. It was the locus of the girl revolution. The women in the industry banded together at the Gathering of the Goddesses, an annual conference to discuss women in snowboarding. Two riders in Boston started a magazine, *Fresh and Tasty* to encourage and inspire girl riders and to showcase their abilities. Suddenly, an identifiable women's scene and style had crystallized, and everyone sat up and took notice.

Tina Basich was one of very few women to attempt the steep jump at the 1997 Winter X-Games. PHOTO PATTY SEGOVIA.

prom

Fine Womens Snowboarding Apparel

Designed by Shannon Dunn, Tina Basich, and Swag

prom/swag • 5651 palmer way, ste. j, carlsbad, ca 92008 send $2 for stickers and info

Prom ad,
Tina and Shannon, 1994.

On a larger scale in America, the identity of "athletic female" was changing. Traditionally, women athletes were either graceful and feminine, as ice skaters or gymnasts, or they were unfeminine, as golfers, tennis players, mountain bikers, or rock climbers. But these and other stereotypes were breaking down in the '90s. Snowboarders like Basich were sexy, feminine, *and* fierce—so fierce, that boys were humbled and girls were offered more varied identities and opportunities as athletes. As role models, Basich and Dunn provided an image for girls to emulate, girls who might never have snowboarded out of the fear of seeming too boyish. Their sensitivity to what girls wanted and their embrace of the do-it-yourself entrepreneurial spirit initiated change and progressive acceptance of women as contributing members in snowboarding's male-oriented culture.

However, Prom's cute, sexy style was coded in two ways. While it empowered many girls to action, distinguishing girls from boys has its down side. Many felt that the girly outfits took the focus away from the riding and placed more emphasis on looks and fashion, which actually turned the clock back for women as athletes. During the new school era, the skate punk mentality invaded snowboarding, exemplified by naked girl graphics and ads. Ironically, the girly style fit in well with the then-prevalent juvenile attitude about gender. Whether hip-hop or hick-inspired, sexist images were flourishing in snowboarding when Prom came out with cute pink or mint-green overalls. For some the images were ironic, for some they weren't. Some girls looked really girly and were snowboarding just to meet boys and be cute. They liked Prom. Some, including Basich and Dunn, had a more ironic attitude about their femininity. They liked Prom, too. Only the way they rode set the two types of girls apart.

Within a year, Basich and Dunn wanted out of the now wildly popular girl scene. They left Swag, taking with them their team manager, Lisa Hudson, and they joined Twist to start their new women's line, which they named Tuesday. "I think Prom had to start out as it did, but we were over it really quickly," says Basich. "I was so against selling snowboarding stuff with images of girls in makeup and no shirts, and a lot of the women-specific companies coming out were using the sex thing to sell, just like the guys. It was hypocritical." With their new line, Tuesday, Basich and Dunn focused more on function. "By that point," says Basich, "the women-specific thing was taking off. There was enough market and momentum within it that the girl style was over. I'm so happy to see that point over with." Soon, gender-identification seemed outdated.

As the girl craze was dying out in snowboarding, it was flourishing in other media. Basich, along with other talented freeriders like Dunn, Morgan Lafonte, Victoria Jealouse, Megan Pischke, and Barrett Christy were getting calls from women's magazines, whose editors, seduced by the strength and beauty of such small women (usually about 5'6", 110 lbs), flocked to feature them. With seven times the circulation of snowboarding magazines, fashion magazines reached a huge new international market of women. One shot in *Seventeen Magazine* could sell more snowboards than a six-page feature in a snowboarding magazine. The mainstream media were quickly recognized as offering an effective marketing tool, and women were recognized as major players.

Inside the snowboarding media, women stopped posing for ads and started riding. Action photos of women increased considerably as the major snowboarding magazines recognized women as high performance riders and as buyers of magazines. Around this same time, video sales were peaking and Victoria Jealouse was becoming a star. In 1994, Mike Hatchett's *Totally Board 2* (*TB2*) came out, and the exclusive boys' club in the big mountain video scene was ruptured by a small girl with big riding skills. Originally a ski racer from Canada, Jealouse was racing snowboards for Burton when she found herself at a Burton photo shoot. The power of image was confirmed: says Jealouse, "One photo of me doing a powder turn at the shoot got me more attention from the industry than winning races ever did. One photo changed everything." She met filmmaker Mike Hatchett and was invited to go to Alaska to shoot *TB2*.

Jealouse followed the tracks of Julie Zell and Bonnie Leary-Zellers, other "extreme" female riders. However, as a rider in Hatchett's films, Jealouse was part of a new generation of freeriders—including Jim Rippey, Noah Salasnek, and Johan Olofsson. Her ability to ride in the dangerous Alaskan backcountry

Shannon Dunn on her first pro model at Mt. Hood, 1994. PHOTO JEFF CURTES.

was informed by her years of experience reading snow conditions and skiing. Big mountain riding was experiencing a renaissance, and Jealouse found herself in the middle of it.

Hatchett's films don't separate men and women riders. They have to ride the same terrain and they are evaluated as equals. "It's really hard always filming with only the best guys," she admits. "They do everything bigger, so even though I'm totally pushing myself, I'm going to look bad next to the boys. I know it's worth it, but I feel like my hands and feet are tied sometimes." Her segments in *TB2–5* gained her a place among the country's most accomplished and adored riders and pushed big mountain riding into the spotlight in the mid '90s.

**Victoria Jealouse, picking a
line in Valdez, Alaska, 1996.**
PHOTO JEFF CURTES.

While Jealouse broke ground for women in the backcountry, Michele Taggart set standards in the half-pipe. She is the consummate competitor. "I was always really low-key when it came to media," says Taggart. "My only focus was doing well so I wouldn't lose my job. Looking back, I realize that people were finding all sorts of ways to make themselves marketable." Taggart grew up in Oregon, became one of Burton's top riders, and won world championship titles for four years in a row during the '90s. Her career trajectory has often been compared to Craig Kelly's. Taggart never had to worry about being media savvy, or cute. She was a winner.

"But I was the girl in the closet at Burton," she says. "I would come out, win a contest, and go back in." After many years, she got sick of life on the circuit. "I asked the people at Burton what I should do if I wanted to film. They said I should go out to Tahoe for a season and hang out with all the film guys. I decided I didn't want to kiss people's asses for a year. That's what it would be. I can understand why the filmers want to be out there traveling with people they like. It's just lame that you could be the best snowboarder in the world but if you don't know 'the dude' that you need to know, you're screwed." Moving from the cut-and-dried world of contests to the more subtle, socially maneuvered realm of freeriding can be rough. Ironically, as the Olympics cause the industry to place more value on a competitive mindset, Taggart wants to move away from competition. "The contest scene is so serious now," she says. "A couple of years ago, the Scandanavians started getting these serious coaches for freestyle. Snowboarders now wake up early, jog, and watch their diet. That's scary." Basich and Dunn popularized a new image for women in snowboarding, and Jealouse pushed boundaries in the backcountry; now Taggart's shift away from her longstanding commitment to competition responds to the shifting landscape of competitive snowboarding in the late '90s.

None of this is to say that Dunn never won contests and Taggart never went freeriding. In fact, Dunn swept many of the contests of the '96–'97 season.

Michele Taggart with *Fresh and Tasty*'s Art Director and Publisher, Melissa Longfellow, at the US Open, Stratton Mountain, Vermont, 1996.
PHOTO GREGG GREENWOOD.

Snowboarding's increasingly mainstream identity is pushing both the athletic and the lifestyle images of its riders, so the leaders of the sport must excel in both areas. Perhaps after the Olympics, riders will have to choose a path: toward the next Olympics, or into freeriding. Either way, women have quite a way to go before they make the same money and can do the same things that men can do. Women like Taggart, Basich, and Jealouse have paved the way for the hundreds of 13- to 14-year-old girls who are getting really good at snowboarding right

now—girls who either don't even think about comparing themselves to boys, or who do, and are better than the boys. Either way, as the ability level of women continues to rise, so do the choices available to them. Women nowadays are encouraged by each other to be themselves and focus on riding more than image.

Michele Taggart, Riksgransen, Sweden, 1997. PHOTO JUSTIN HOSTYNEK.

The Northwest is sort of out of the trend loop in a way. There are fewer influences here, so everything is sort of function before fashion. That's a very Northwest vibe. Big mountain riding is in fashion right now and there are a lot of big mountains in the Northwest. It's like the trend came to us.

—Rob Morrow, CEO, Morrow Snowboards

We never ran ads. First it was because we had no money. Then it was because we didn't think it really worked. We started doing ads for Gnu and still sold equal amounts of Gnus and Lib Techs. It was an experiment and ads lost.

—Mike Olson, CEO, Mervin Manufacturing

Boeing, beer, pot, coffee, snowboarding, music, Microsoft.

—Mike Olson, CEO, Mervin Manufacturing

A lot of the new schoolers who were into speed like Noah Salasnek and Jamie Lynn . . . they were the ones who made a mockery of slow speed jibbing. As soon as they all learned to snowboard that all went away. It was a way for skaters who couldn't snowboard yet to fake it.

—Tom Sims, pioneer

I certainly saw snowboarding and music explode hand in hand in Seattle, and a lot of the bands snowboarded. I think the mainstream came to snowboarding, more than snowboarding reached out to the mainstream. Of course now, the music and snowboarding industries are pretty cognitive of the fact that they're selling to the mainstream, and they market and produce accordingly.

—Jeff Galbraith, Senior Editor, *Snowboarder Magazine*

There will always be that MBHC that only want snowy days and no media.

—Damian Sanders, pro

You never see park shots anymore, because nobody wants to be seen in parks.

—Ken Block, CEO, Circus Distribution

I don't think fashion is as important now as it was in the new school era. Now that it's so huge and diverse, it's all inclusive again. A few years ago, to be a snowboarder, a nerdy kid would have to go shopping and buy hair dye and try to belong. Now, I see kids in one-piece ski outfits on the hill and it's cool. It doesn't matter anymore.

—Tina Basich, pro

It's the whole laid back attitude. It comes from Jamie Lynn, the Cummins brothers, Todd Schlosser, Dave Lee, a bunch of people just ripping but not screaming about it.

—Trevor Graves, photographer

I feel like in the Northwest you just sit on the chair and make fun of the wusses who wouldn't ride in bad weather.

—Rob Morrow, CEO, Morrow Snowboards

I remember when Jim Rippey came out with Hatchett and me to Alaska for the first time and hucked right off this cliff we were all jumping and he just beatered down the whole thing. For the rest of the day, he just sat and watched. He was humbled and took the time to learn what we did.

—Tom Burt, pro

When people see the videos of people making sick powder turns in Alaska, they want that. It's a fantasy. Most people aren't educated enough to be out there. Now with commercial heli being so popular, people are getting dropped in places that they are not prepared to be riding in.

—Jeff Fulton, pro

If I didn't have a family, I'd be a snowboard bum, cruising around, crashing wherever. Oh, but then I wouldn't be able to afford helicopter rides. Forget it.

—Tom Sims, pioneer

ELEVEN BACK TO THE COUNTRY

FULL CIRCLE

AS THE '90S RACED ON, SNOWBOARD-
ING WAS IN THE PROCESS OF FINDING
ITSELF, ONCE AGAIN, REDEFINING ITS
IDENTITY AGAINST ITS OWN OVER-
HYPED SKATEBOARDING-INFUSED
IMAGE. THE NEW SCHOOL JIBBER IMAGE
THAT STUCK IN THE MAINSTREAM PUB-
LIC IMAGINATION PORTRAYED SNOW-
BOARDERS AS BADLY BEHAVED PUNKS,
BUT SNOWBOARDERS WERE REJECTING

Tom Burt at Teton
Pass, Wyoming.
PHOTO AARON SEDWAY.

the played-out, over-hyped caricature of themselves. Snowboarding had become pure image, manufactured and mediated to the point where the "soul" of snowboarding seemed to have evaporated. While alternative culture, technical skate tricks, and the SoCal infrastructure built a successful mediagenic machine out of snowboarding, many of the sport's leaders were restless, uncomfortable with what now felt artificial. They sought a regrounding, a new source of respect. Where could they find it? The X-Games? The snowboard parks? *Rolling Stone Magazine*? Instead of looking outward, snowboarding took a look at itself to figure out how snowboarding was different from its influences. The answer was found in the mountains.

The quest for soul takes us back to what sets snowboarding apart from all the hype, back to where it all started: the backcountry. In the early days, snowboarders were forced to hike in the backcountry because they weren't allowed on the lifts. Now, not only are snowboarders allowed on the lifts, but they're everywhere, tracking out the tree runs, blasting music in the snowboard parks, vibing each other and everyone else. Now, people head for the backcountry to get away from, not to be with other snowboarders. "When the backlash came against jibbing," says backcountry expert Tom Burt, " the media shifted to what people thought was cool, and that was freeriding, using the terrain that's in front of you." Hiking and freeriding in the quiet, untouched natural setting places more emphasis on one's relationship with nature than with any social scene. As the new school image became more and more of a joke, backcountry and big terrain riding moved from it's marginal position to the center of the snowboarding media limelight.

"Extreme" All Over Again

Of course people had been riding outside the resorts throughout the new school era. The term "extreme" in this context referred to a certain discipline of riding, developed in conjunction with extreme skiing in the late '80s. In the early '90s, extreme snowboarding established into its own settled subculture with a small

Adam Hostetter and Jeremy Jones in Valdez with Standard Films, 1996. PHOTO JEFF CURTES.

group of heroes, including Shawn Farmer, Matt Goodwill, Steve Klassen, and Julie Zell. These riders and others gathered for an annual "King of the Hill" Extreme Contest to test their daring and skill in the home of big, dangerous terrain, Alaska. Extreme riders are physically different than freestyle pros, four or five inches taller, with more bulk on them, so that they can ride a longer, stiffer type of board. They are mostly mountaineers, who spend years learning about snow conditions and behavior, weather patterns, emergency techniques, and rock climbing. In other words, they are not the type of people who would go to a 311 show in a Huntington Beach parking lot.

With a renewed interest in big mountain riding came a new appreciation for the value of experience. Tom Burt, one of the original Avalanche riders, had been snowboarding and skiing on tricky terrain for twenty years. This kind of constant and varied experience put him on a level above most other extreme riders. "The thing about the backcountry," says Burt, "is that snowboarding has put a lot of people out in situations that they weren't ready for." One of the great secrets to snowboarding's success is that one can feel comfortable on a snowboard within a few days. "That's the difference between snowboarding and skiing," he continues. "Skiing takes longer to learn, so that by the time you learn to ski well, you can also read the snow pretty well. You can't fake experience." Tom Burt's high speed and elegant lines, which he had been perfecting for ten years, were admired as though new by the younger generation of snowboarders in the mid-'90s.

Videos glamorized big mountain riding. Mike Hatchett's films especially changed the way the public thought about snowboarding. Hatchett started making films in 1991, with Mike McIntire (Mac Dawg). McIntire was a skate videomaker and slipped right into the skate-heavy side of snowboarding. "Big mountain riding was sort of marginal for a while there," says Hatchett. "When we did *TB2* and *TB3*, it seemed like it was the full new school jibber, total fashion thing; wide stance, baggy thing. It was a great, new thing at the time, but it kind of worked its way out." Hatchett and McIntire collaborated on *TB2* and *3*; McIntire

would do his skate-influenced section and Hatchett his big mountain section. As a rock climber and mountaineer, Hatchett's real interest and specialty is big terrain filming, which was becoming more and more popular. "I think the jib thing got oversaturated and people got sick of it," says Hatchett. "It was so over publicized, the word 'jib' almost became a joke." Hatchett's films were soon regarded as the showcase for the best riders around. They fostered and demonstrated excellence in freeriding.

"It's hard to portray how difficult a 720 is on a snowboard, but a huge cliff is a huge cliff, and more people enjoy it: old surfers, ski bums, and older people can relate to it more than spinning," Hatchett explains. Snowboarding's common ties with surfing came to the fore again as the urban skate vibe subsided. This new era threw the door open again to people who were put off by the kid culture of the new school. "I hope my movies help people to respect big mountain riding," says Hatchett. While respect could be gained through spinning tricks in the new school era, skaters and other critics later came down on snowboarding as a rip-off of skating. Progressive riders saw the difficulty of the big mountain as not only a challenge, but a challenge that skaters could not scoff at or condemn as simply imitation. It also separated the novices from those who had been around longer. The new core was the group that could prove their worth on the steeps. Credibility was found on the mountain, not in the park.

But the new era wasn't just a roots movement; each era takes something with it, and the stakes of extreme riding were being raised. "When freestylers learned to freeride, freeriding became much more exciting to watch and more popular," says Tina Basich. "Instead of just dropping off of huge cliffs, people like Noah Salasnek were doing tricks off of cliffs. It was better than freestyle and better than extreme riding. The fusion was awesome." It wasn't until the synthesis of freestyle and extreme riding that the media and the public could embrace big mountain riding. Hatchett's films boosted the freeriding careers of Jim Rippey, Noah Salasnek, Victoria Jealouse, Johan Olofsson, and many others. Parts of TB films became legendary: Rippey's brushes with death are famous; Olofsson's 3,000 foot descent in 35 seconds became a page in everyone's reference book of amazing feats. The mediagenic culture of freestyle fused with the earnest personality of mountaineering to form a new image for snowboarding, more mature than freestyle, more dynamic than extreme.

Todd Franzen, Jason Rasmus (J2), and Jason Ford in Juneau, Alaska, 1997. PHOTO JEFF CURTES.

Big mountain riding was downright dangerous. Avalanches, sluffs, helicopter crashes, crevasses, rocks, and exposure to the elements were taking their toll on those who either weren't prepared or were unlucky. *Medium* magazine's 1996 Death Issue addressed the consequences of snowboarding's move into the realm of stunt riding. An only slightly tongue-in-cheek article entitled, "To Die

For? Has Snowboarding Gone Too Far?" accused the media of making big mountain riding seem too easy: "Some classic lessons being taught by this group included: 'Bigger is always better'; 'Avalanches can be outrun'; and 'No matter how many rocks you tumble through, you'll never hit one.'" The magazine took a poll, asking "Who is the snowboarder most likely to die?" Jim Rippey won with 42% of the vote. Rippey's fearless and determined riding straddled the line between talent and insanity.

A New Home

Nowadays, everyone is on a quest for the most out of the way spot, the most varied terrain, the least-mediated mountains. While Alaska represents the ultimate journey into the unknown, the Northwestern US has emerged as the counterculture to the SoCal scene, and Seattle has become the new home of snowboarding. "The environment breeds style and culture," says Mervin (Mike Olson's company, including Gnu and Lib Tech) team manager, Paul Ferrel. "The Northwest people laugh at the stereotype SoCal types who come up for the Banked Slalom and biff on the steeps." The Northwest tradition inevitably goes back to Craig Kelly and the original Mount Baker Hard Core. In the '80s, Kelly and others had to leave the Northwest to be noticed. Ironically, the media is now finding its way to the Cascades more often, and many riders have moved there to gain freeriding experience, skill, and now even media coverage, during the second half of the '90s.

As focus pulled away from the hype cluster, snowboard companies like Ride and Sims moved their headquarters to Seattle, and native Northwest outfits, like K2, Mervin, and Morrow, became major players. It's no surprise that snowboarding now finds a home in the Northwest. Seattle and Portland seem to be a hotbed for cultural production, where all things '90s find their home: grunge music, independent film, microbrewed beer, Starbucks coffee, Microsoft, and Nike. Ironically, the Northwest's "out of the way" identity has drawn everyone in and all but erased itself. Even Tim Pogue, after leaving Ride, chose Seattle as the site for his new 10,000-square-foot snow sports megastore *cum* museum, Faction, where he plans to immortalize the hand and foot prints of famous snowboarders in cement, à la Hollywood Boulevard.

"The snowboarding scene there is just like [the independent record label] Sub-Pop," says *Transworld Snowboarding* editor, Billy Miller. "The whole Sub-Pop thing is about irony, 'I'm so out of it, I'm cool.' That is so Seattle. It's far from the media hubs, and it's cool in that 'out of it' way. That's how snowboarders are here too. They don't spray about how good they are, they just go out and get really good. Then they act all self-deprecating and quiet." Miller left the *Transworld* hub in Southern California to work from a home office in Portland. Just as the media came to Seattle with the mainstreaming of grunge, press attention turned to Northwest riders and ski areas as big mountain terrain became more popular.

The increasing recognition of Northwest riders influenced the whole pro snow-boarder identity. Many cite Jamie Lynn, a pro from Auburn, Washington who rides for Lib Tech, as the quintessential rider of today. "Jamie Lynn is a nice, polite person and has no crazy ego," says Henry Hester, a prominent snow-board-maker in Southern California, who used to be based in Seattle. "When all the pros get together at Mount Hood in the summer, the kids go and are influenced so strongly by these pros. Jamie Lynn, and others with the same positive, Northwest attitude influenced kids so that they were polite and cool and still radical, more radical than you and more nice than you." If Shaun Palmer is a rock star, Jamie Lynn is a super hero. Both are amazing riders, but while Palmer was at the top in the late '80s, when snowboarding was still trying to get attention, Lynn was at the top during a peak of snowboarding popularity in the main-stream, and at a moment when snowboarders were trying to separate them-selves from the oversaturated snowboarder image.

Burly big mountain riders
Tex Devenport and Matt
Goodwill. PHOTO TREVOR GRAVES.

Ian Ruhter, classic road gap in South Lake Tahoe.
PHOTO COURTESY BUD FAWCETT.

Josh Dirksen, Mt. Baker,
Washington, 1997.
PHOTO TREVOR GRAVES.

As snowboarding's tide turned north to the mountains, it was finding its own identity away from the skaters and the style hubs of Southern California. *Snowboarder* editor and Washington native Jeff Galbraith agrees: "A lot of the Southern California appeal was about lifestyle more than sport," he says. "You cannot take snowboarding to the next level in Southern California. Many who wanted to go further, moved away. Those who didn't care about the next level stayed in Southern California." Snowboarding, in a sense, was growing up.

Snowboarding has taken people and pushed them along, which is a good thing and the FIS [Fédération International du Ski] is probably going to take that away. They are going to kill the potential of someone who should be in the Olympics. The first ones won't be that way but after '98 it will be that way. To go to the Olympics you have to give up your clothing sponsor, all your sponsors, except your board. NO stickers or anything. There will be a team clothing sponsor, who will give the FIS a million dollars. The Olympics as an idea is a great thing. The reality is sort of a bummer. Anyone who wants to go to the Olympics next time will have to be with the FIS, training for the next four years, which means being on tour competing all season.

—Tom Burt, pro

The only way to stop the FIS from ruining snowboarding is to get the athletes to realize that it all comes down to leverage control of the calendar and the athletes. The dollars all get filtered through the political bureaucracy. To qualify, you need a certain number of points, and to get them you have to go to all the competitions, which means spend all your time out of the country.

—Jake Burton, Founder and President, Burton Snowboards

Now we are just leaving this lengthy era of contest hating. With the Olympics, the pendulum will swing in the other direction. To be a major pro, riders will have to compete. This will be expensive for a company, sending someone on a pro circuit is much more expensive than sending them on a few shoots. It will be harder to be a small company.

—Tom Sims, CEO, Sims Sports

That's what I think is so cool about snowboarding. It teaches you that you can be who you want to be. Anyone can do it and everyone can have their own style. When I think of the Olympics, I get worried. Sometimes I think of the Olympics as a scary thing. I'm glad I got to be in snowboarding before now. Will kids look at the Olympic gold medalist and say I want that and then go and train for 4 years?

—Tina Basich, pro

Now that snowboarding is more accepted by the public and more legitimate, the moms are getting all overbearing, just like with all of those Olympic sports. These 14-year-old kids are getting so pushed and by the time they're 19, they'll hate snowboarding.

—Jeff Fulton, pro

I like competition. I wasn't sure why I liked it so much but now I know why. I want to go to the Olympics, win a gold medal, be the first snowboarder to win a gold medal and be written about in the history books. That's what it all really comes down to.

—Jimi Scott, pro

The Olympics will change the sport altogether. I didn't get into snowboarding to go to the Olympics. I don't think it sounds so great. Snowboarding is great because it's different from other sports. Now it will get too serious, training, competing, training, working out in gyms. There's nothing wrong with all of that, but snowboarding isn't like that, and it'll be sad when it becomes like that.

—Cara Beth Burnside, pro

I think that the Olympics are way too big and they are going to change snowboarding. They are making us fit into their mold. They aren't fitting into our mold. It will create a reality for snowboarding that millions will swallow and accept.

—Morgan Lafonte, pro

There's no cultural relevance to the Olympics. It's anticulture.

—Lee Crane, Editor, *Snowboarding Online*

Olympics are just another 5-minute window to the world.

—Billy Miller, Senior Editor, *Transworld Snowboarding*

It's gonna be just like the dream team at the end anyway. They'll decide at the last five minutes and all the rock stars will be there.

—Trevor Graves, photographer

Somebody yelled, "Go USA!" in the pipe yesterday, and everybody was like, "UGH."

—Jake Burton, the day after the '97 US Open

PHOTO RICH VAN EVERY.

TWELVE OLYMPICS AND ITS (POSSIBLE) IMPACT

WHAT DOES IT MEAN?

IN DECEMBER OF 1994, AS SNOW-
BOARDERS WERE GETTING KICKED OFF
OF BRECKENRIDGE FOR WEARING GUNS,
THE INTERNATIONAL OLYMPIC
COMMITTEE DECIDED TO INCLUDE
SNOWBOARIDNG IN THE 1998 WINTER
OLYMPICS IN NAGANO, JAPAN. HYPE?
OH, YES. SNOWBOARDERS FROM
AROUND THE WORLD WOULD COMPETE
IN BOTH HALF-PIPE AND SLALOM EVENTS,

and not just as an exhibition sport, but for medals. Should snowboarders be cheering or sneering? By the time this decision was announced in '94, snowboarding culture had gotten to a point where competition not only was not important, it was a dirty word. Would the top riders now have to have one coach, wake up early, get drug tested, and wear some red, white, and blue uniforms to light the torch in a Coke commercial? Or would there be a scowling photo of a disheveled Todd Richards or Terje Haakonsen on Wheaties boxes?

Many snowboarders secretly hope the Olympics would have to bow in some way to snowboarding, but doubtless, the Olympics will have more impact on the sport than vice versa. But how? How does a super established, mainstream, international, heavily televised, and universally watched contest affect a little old subculture that has made it big on a smallish scale? To understand how the cultural clash of the Olympics and snowboarding was playing out in the years between the IOC decision and the Games in Japan, a certain amount of dry organizational information in necessary. First, two main governing bodies jockeyed for the right to qualify and choose riders to go to the games: the International Snowboard Federation (ISF), a group of snowboarders who had been developing an international circuit for eight years (the ISF tour is run by snowboarders, for snowboarders, but it is unsubsidized, and therefore more expensive to compete on), and the Fédération Internacional du Ski (FIS), the skiing organization that had already organized all the Olympic snow sports.

The FIS had a bad reputation among snowboarders and skiers for being militaristic and closed minded, while the ISF was known to have the snowboarders' interests at heart. Even though the ISF circuit is a whole lot more pricey than the FIS circuit, for freestyle riders, the opportunity to express their individuality was worth it. The cloning process that goes on for the FIS was out of the question for freestyle snowboarders, who valued their freedom of identity. Unfortunately, the main reason the Committee decided to debut snowboarding ahead of surfing and other sports that had been jockeying for years was that snowboarding could be controlled by the FIS as a discipline of skiing.

A *discipline* of *skiing* ??

Almost everyone in the industry was horrified to find that to go to the Olympics, a rider had to be a member of the Ski Federation. Many believed that the Olympics threatened the sport's integrity. However, most who were good enough to go wanted to go. Thus snowboarding unintentionally set its course for Japan.

Snowboarding's tentative relationship with the Olympics mirrors its relationship to the mainstream in general. The contradiction that pervades snowboarding's history: getting big and still staying small. "The Olympics are a fascinating little microcosm of the whole mainstreaming fear," says *Snowboarder* publisher, Doug Palladini. "We've always shied away from the political structure, the rigidity, and all the things in competition that don't really apply to the concept of our sport. But having the opportunity to go to the Olympics has made all the riders reassess what they want to do. When an opportunity like this comes along, you're not so prone to being a cool guy, you just want to go." It's hard to scoff at the Olympics. A gold medal represents an accomplishment that not many snowboarders ever imagined could be within their grasp.

A renewed focus on athleticism brought contests back from the dead in the years leading up to the Games. But the contests had changed in the interim. Riders now win up to $45K for first place in a half-pipe event. Decent pipes and jumps were built and organizers were forced to think about the riders, not just the TV cameras. New events like boardercross, slopestyle, and big air satisfy the evolving interests of snowboarders and the public. Many snowboarders who excel in the new formats find that contests are a more agreeable and direct way to make money than playing media politics as a freerider.

The industry was also getting more established and more conservative; the small, core companies that flooded the market throughout the '90s started going bankrupt in '96, while major ski companies like K2 were gaining larger market share.

Now in 1997, growth is happening outside the prime male teenage demographic. Families look to mainstream companies they already know and trust rather than to the snowboarding companies that have been around for years, but have been unknown outside the culture. This kind of trust will doubtless intensify after the Olympics, when the demographic widens even more.

So, it turns out snowboarding was getting ready for the Olympics, after all. What effect the Games will ultimately have on the sport, we can only guess. Snowboarders, especially pros, see more potential for harm than good. What will happen to professional snowboarding when there are Olympic medalists? Will there be a huge split between those who want to go to the next Olympics and those who don't? Or will the Games just be another five-minute window to the world for snowboarding, over and forgotten by the following season? It's supposed to be the third most media-covered sport at the Games, right behind figure skating and downhill skiing. Surely that kind of exposure will have some impact on who will be riding and how they will ride as snowboarding and its culture enter the twenty-first century.

CONCLUSION WHAT HAPPENS WHEN A SUBCULTURE GOES MAINSTREAM?

I REMEMBER SEEING A PHOTO A FEW YEARS AGO IN *TRANSWORLD SNOWBOARDING*—IT WAS OF DAN QUAYLE, STANDING TRIUMPHANTLY ON A SNOWBOARD. THE CAPTION READ, "NOW IT'S REALLY OVER."

OF COURSE IT WASN'T. CULTURE DOESN'T GO DOWN THAT EASILY. IT HAS ITS OWN DECENTRALIZED AND CHAOTIC PATH, dependent on no single influence. Even if the top keeps getting more commercialized and mainstream, subculture just keeps breeding underneath, like a bunch of cool bugs on the underside of an old log.

The mainstreaming and "demise" of snowboarding is one of the most discussed topics of the past ten years. Certainly the industry is having its share of shake-ups. Over the last few seasons, hundreds of independent, snowboarder-owned snowboard shops have been pushed out of business by large chain sporting goods stores. Snowboarder-owned manufacturers have been either bought out or pushed out of business by the rising stakes of the consolidating industry. Why? Economics. Bigger companies can absorb more loss and provide better price points, and all the sweat and integrity in the world can't stop it.

Corporate procedure is itself evolving, learning from the finicky youth market and the smaller "core" companies that won the kids' loyalty. Big companies now know that to succeed in seeming authentic, they have to hire credibility—insiders—to run their snowboarding divisions. But corporate culture still has a ways to go. Will the head of Nike's imminent snowboarding line be around in five years? ten years? twenty years? That's how long the pioneers have been in the game. Even a hired insider won't have the stamina for twenty years of corporate politics and each time people turn over in a company, a little bit of soul is lost.

The last issue of *Time Magazine* (June 9, 1997) said that my generation, once dismissed as vapid and lazy, is now a bunch of entrepreneurial go-getters. It's true, we're growing up and bringing our childhood games with us. But that's nothing new. The pioneers were the original slackers, refusing to let go of their childhood games, which was much more daring back in the '70s. They were labeled dreamers, we're labeled entrepreneurial go-getters. The difference is that now, those games are official culture, sanctioned, and profitable.

Most of those original boardmakers are still making boards and snowboarding today. To them, and the majority of the industry, including the snowboard media, pros, photographers, and clothing/equipment makers, snowboarding is not a job. It really is a way of life. These people do what they do so that they can live snowboarding, not just live off of it. That's the difference between big business and snowboarding, for the moment, anyway. I've learned a lot from the people who grew up inside snowboarding. People like Mike Olson, Brad Steward, and many others (I could fill a page with names) have made successful lives out of what they loved to do most. They have enabled snowboarding's rise and in turn been enabled by snowboarding to create and pursue their dreams. Their lives have been an inspiration to me, and provide examples of successful cultural entrepreneurship for others.

In bridging snowboarding's past and future, maybe our efforts are best spent making sure the kids know how this all happened—what kind of values snowboarding emerged from and how it evolved: how it was developed and fought for against all odds by a group of people who, along with inventing equipment, riding styles and gear, also nurtured a set of values: rebelliousness, free-mindedness, subversion, glamour, irony, and authenticity. If the kids understand the history, they might be more selective about the marketing hype, corporate influence, and heavy consumerism that's thrown their way. This book is only one effort in that direction. Doubtless, more will follow and provide an array of perspectives on the culture. I look forward to reading them. Almost as much as I look forward to next season.